The
Cross-Country Skier's
Bible

ERWIN A. BAUER

The Cross-Country
Skier's Bible

With a Section on Snowshoeing

DOUBLEDAY & COMPANY, INC.
GARDEN CITY, NEW YORK
1977

Library of Congress Cataloging in Publication Data

Bauer, Erwin A
The cross-country skier's bible.

Bibliography: p. 124
Includes index.
1. Cross-country skiing—United States.   2. Cross-country skiing—Canada.   3. Snowshoes and snowshoeing—United States.   4. Snowshoes and snowshoeing—Canada.
I. Title.
GV854.9.C7B37   796.9′3′0973
ISBN: 0-385-01321-3
Library of Congress Catalog Card Number 76–52001

CONTENTS

The
Cross-Country Skier's
Bible

Cross-country skiing is possible wherever enough snow falls in winter—in deepest wildernesses or near home. ERWIN A. BAUER.

INTRODUCTION

During the past decade or so, a new kind of skiing—in, fact, a whole new sport—has caught on in the United States and Canada. It has nothing to do with speed and acrobatics, with crowds, ski resorts, and high fashion. Nor is it a temporary craze. Instead here is a more gentle, quiet game that depends on the solitude and the extraordinary hush of winter in lonely, beautiful places. The miracle is that cross-country skiing—some call it ski touring, ski running, or Nordic skiing did not take hold a long, long time ago.

Somebody referred to touring as "skiing à la carte, from a rich menu long and varied, filled with quiet delights." You participate as casually or as seriously as you like; either way it is a physical conditioner without equal among all sports. There is no need to depend on ski lifts and well-manicured slopes because you make your own way wherever you go. Crowded parking lots and waiting lines are not part of the picture, nor is your wallet emptied all too soon, as on typical downhill skiing holidays. In other words, cross-country skiing has everything. Someone described its recent "discovery" by outdoorsmen as "the quiet revolution."

Although still in its infancy in the New World, cross-country skiing is really many centuries old. The origin of skis, snowshoes, and similar devices for traveling across winter landscapes is lost in prerecorded history. But without doubt the use of skis/snowshoes began in subarctic Eurasia, where the human inhabitants needed some kind of foot extender to help them travel across deep snow.

We know that a kind of crude snowshoe was used about 4000 B.C. in central Asia. This same device evolved gradually into the webbed snowshoe that found its way via a land bridge (which once existed over the Bering Strait) to what is now Alaska and all northern North America. Much more obscure is who used the first skis as we know them now, and when. But surely the place was Scandinavia, where skis have been worn during all the winters of written history there. In fact, the word "ski" comes from the old Norse *skith*.

The first skis were merely slats or shingles of any shape that could be split from wood and somehow fastened onto the feet. The best guess is that they were fashioned from European birch, the hardwood that happened to be handiest. From crude wooden slivers came the long, smooth runners we know today. The development has been almost imperceptibly slow, but is certainly quickening right now.

For hundreds of years skis were merely a means of transportation, but by 1747 they had become military weapons as well. That's when Norway fielded the first known ski troops. Now most modern armies maintain elite ski squadrons, and ski soldiers could play important roles in the looming future conflict for precious natural resources located in polar portions of the earth. Interestingly, the cross-country skiing event that attracts most attention in recent world Olympiads is the biathlon, which combines skill both in skiing and shooting.

Because skiing was fun as well as work, it also became an important recreation in northern and alpine Europe. Scandinavian immigrants introduced the sport to America, but it never attracted much attention here until the 1930s. Since then its growing popularity has been extraordinary; today no corner of the United States snow belt (as well as some corners well outside) are without ski resorts and slopes. The near mania for skiing has become so important that new industries, whole communities, and radically changed life styles have developed from it.

However, America's big ski boom only encompassed downhill or alpine skiing. It had nothing to do with the less glamorous kind, in which a person propelled himself over the snow. True enough, there always existed a small hard core of cross-country skiers in the United States, most of them being concentrated in the Northeast. But it wasn't until the mid-1960s that a change was noticeable.

Maybe it was no coincidence that Americans learned about ski touring at the same time they were making other crucial discoveries. Suddenly it was apparent that many of our resources, including fuel, were in short supply. The quality of life was being eroded. For the first time there was a genuine concern for the American environment, and it was evident that we were headed nowhere —and fast. That was surely an ideal time for an unhurried, unstructured, and contemplative sport to catch on. That was also when one Rudolph Franz Mattesich came into the picture.

An ex-officer in the Hungarian Army, Mattesich had immigrated to the United States after World War I with little more to his name than a skill in skiing and fencing. For a while he survived by teaching the latter in Chicago. Later he participated in an Austrian Government travel bureau that encouraged Americans to go skiing in Austria—downhill, of course. But all the time he was ski touring and spreading the gospel of the long, thin ski to a few close friends. Then came the 1950s, and a mild new interest in physical fitness swept the nation. That planted an idea with Mattesich.

With a few associates and encouragement from the President's Council on Physical Fitness, Rudy Mattesich founded the Ski Touring Council in 1962. Its purpose was "to revive the sport of cross-country skiing in America." Today the Council has more than a hundred active, enthusiastic members (professional and amateur) and publishes an annual guide to touring in the East. It organizes trips, workshops, and classes. Activity was, until recently, concentrated in the Northeast, but there is now even greater ski-touring fervor in the West, with emphasis on the Rocky Mountains, the High Sierras, and the Cascade regions.

Even the resorts that grew and thrived on the artificial glamor and thrills of lift-served downhill skiing have taken a new look at the situation. Many of the most prosperous resorts have started ski-touring instruction, have hired guides, and have provided special facilities.

One resort manager in Utah who had wisely opened up a rental shop for cross-country equipment made a discovery that is commonplace now. "Skiers come in here," he noted, "and try rental skis, boots, and poles for the novelty of it. But next day they can't wait to get back to the shop to buy their own stuff. Some are even more selective—more critical—than when they are shopping for downhill gear."

There are a good many factors behind the steady rise of cross-country skiing. Escape—getting away from crowds, confusion, noise, artificiality—is certainly one of them. After a time spent around a popular downhill resort, some winter-sport buffs develop a great yearning for something less contrived, less hectic, and less social.

Cost is also a factor, especially in inflated times. A skiing trip is not a venture to be planned on a modest budget, and many skiers can't even consider a trip that would make them live as paupers the rest of the year. The cost of lift tickets alone during a ski season is enough to make many potential skiers blanch.

Changing psychology in the late 1970s has been another, more subtle factor. Skiing in the United States has always been a social-status activity as well as an exhilarating sport. Many "skiers" have gone to winter resorts simply because it was the thing to do, without any intention of risking the slopes. At least one recent survey suggests that the need to be seen at Vail, Aspen, Sun Valley, or Alta isn't nearly as great nowadays, especially not for younger skiers.

Touring is attracting many fans who are afraid of downhill speed and possible injury. Probably most in this group are older people, but they quickly discover that the sport has its own rewards. The touring skis, for instance, are narrow, easy to use, and only a third the weight of alpine skis. The boots also are lightweight and snug-

Cross-country skiing is a test and competition for many. Here skiers begin a three-mile race at Sun Valley, Idaho. SUN VALLEY NEWS BUREAU PHOTO.

Among the greatest satisfactions of any winter is ski touring out across fresh, unbroken snow. COLORADO SKI COUNTRY.

For many, skiing is also the means to explore—to head for the mountains with a backpack and thereby see lonely places all others miss. ERWIN A. BAUER.

fitting. Bindings are uncomplicated and fit into the ski by toe alone, whereas plastic downhill bindings lock the foot to the ski and forbid free movement of a skier's heel. And a complete set of the finest ski-touring equipment costs less than half a so-so outfit for downhill slopes.

Then, to replace the nervous uncertainty of a steep downhill run, there is the undiluted physical pleasure of the basic touring motion—something between a walk and a gentle jog, which soon becomes a smooth glide. It is easy to learn, and anyone with modest co-ordination and of any age can soon be eating up snow-covered distance with grace and balance he may never have realized he had.

This isn't to say that all ski touring is one glorious glide over a stunning winter landscape. It gets complicated if you want to make it that way. Instead of just a stimulating ski-hike on a Sunday afternoon, you can stretch it out (with training, planning, and experience, of course) into a weekend jaunt or a camping trip even longer than that. Or you can take up cross-country racing. In later chapters, we'll show how skiing can be a means to countless other goals, to exploring, timber cruising, trapping, hunting, fishing, photography, and bird and wildlife watching. Like any other physical activity, cross-country skiing also stimulates challenge. And competition.

To dispel any thought that Nordic skiing is only for persons suffering from vertigo, consider the following. Racing in three World Ski Championships and three winter Olympiads in the 1950s and 1960s, Sixten Jernberg of Sweden won eight gold, three silver, and four bronze medals in grueling events up to fifty kilometers. He might be considered the greatest cross-country performer to date, and one of the greatest of all athletes. What other athletics can match those medals? And how about the several skiers who every winter ski all the way across the total, absolute winter wilderness of Yellowstone National Park? There are no other skiers here to spark extra competitive effort, and no money, glory, or gold medallions to reward first finishers. On the other hand, it is a dramatic, live-or-die contest against high altitudes, subzero days, and even colder nights; for over a hundred miles the skier's only chance to arrive safely is within himself.

However, for the purposes of most ski tourers, and for readers of this book, cross-country skiing is not a race against time or against other skiers, or with life and death in the balance. Rather, it is just the best and most complete sport that humans have yet devised to enjoy winter in our wonderful land.

My wife Peggy and I are free-lance writers and photographers, field editors of *Outdoor Life* mag-

Among the many dividends of ski touring anywhere during midwinter is the incomparable opportunity of seeing native wildlife at close range, such as (TOP) this bull elk in Yellowstone Park, (BELOW RIGHT) the pair of male moose in Jackson Hole, and (BELOW LEFT) mule deer fawn on a snowy hillside. ERWIN A. BAUER.

Author and wife Peggy in winter camp in the Tetons. ERWIN A. BAUER.

azine, and concerned mostly with outdoor sports and travel, high adventure, nature, and the environment. All this permits us to be based in Jackson Hole, Wyoming, which must be included among the most beautiful places on this planet. If there is a drawback in our arrangement, it is in the nearly fatal attraction of what I can see beyond the office window: open sagebrush flats giving way abruptly to the Teton Mountains. At any season it is far more exciting to be out there than indoors pounding a typewriter, but especially after snow blankets the landscape.

So we've worked out a routine. Call it a discipline. We work hard during the morning and maybe for a while into the early afternoon. Then, after lunch, we clamp on the cross-country skis and head out in almost any direction. Our experiences in doing that are what ski touring is all about. With local variations, almost any skier can duplicate them elsewhere.

One direction we might take is toward the Gros Ventre River, which hurries nearby to join the Snake, the main water artery of the Jackson Hole country. That means that we ski across a portion of Grand Teton National Park land, which is trailless—unless we happen to follow our own ski tracks of previous days. Here is level landscape over which we can make good speed but do not always want to.

Coyote tracks are certain to intersect our path, although we seldom see the animals that make them. But the dark object looming ahead in a snow drift is almost certain to be a bull moose bedded down for the afternoon, conserving energy during periods of intense cold. The animal has seen us many times, and unless we glide too close, it will not even stand up to acknowledge our presence. But it is not the only moose we will meet, because many migrate down from the mountains to spend the winter months in these bottoms.

We may see much other wildlife, such as a bald eagle (rare elsewhere) perched on a dead snag overlooking the Snake, which never completely freezes. Sometimes, late in the afternoon, we will meet a flock of sage grouse hurrying ghostlike over the snow to a roosting site, or a band of mule deer, which are much more shy than the moose.

But mostly Peggy and I just savor the total tranquillity and exquisite beauty of winter in northwestern Wyoming. Only rarely hereabouts do we encounter another human, and if so he will be a skier or snowshoer on some similar mission of escape. In summertime this region is crowded with people who have come from all over America to inspect the great natural beauty. But not now. Except in those areas where snowmobilers seem to gather, the region belongs to anyone who will get out on cross-country skis. Or snowshoes. And it isn't vastly different in snow country anywhere.

Besides giving us chances of savoring what we see along the way, our afternoon ski tours are immensely invigorating, mentally and physically. Disagreements with editors, publishers, and other personal problems seem to evaporate with a good workout. And there is no denying that too many of us spend too much of our winters sitting on our behinds and thereby getting out of shape. There are statistics aplenty to prove that regular cross-country skiing is a better conditioner than swimming or jogging, cycling or alpine skiing, tennis or golf.

In this case physical fitness does not refer to massive muscular development and great strength. Far from it. Instead it refers to how well a body performs, for instance how heart and lungs co-operate to make muscles function. Ski touring has a considerable advantage in that it thoroughly exercises *all* of a person's major muscle groups—those of arms, legs, back, abdomen, and chest.

We now know (also from numerous studies and compiled statistics) that a high level of physical fitness provides protection against heart attacks. Ski running is also an aerobic activity, which means it is excellent for controlling weight; regular skiing rapidly uses up body fat. Girl watching is nowhere better than along a ski touring trail, because you never meet anyone who has skied very seriously who is also chubby. There is something especially appealing about a lithe and limber person gliding effortlessly along a quiet ski trail.

So there you have cross-country skiing summed up. It is exhilarating to the senses. There is a sudden new awareness of your own body and skills. It's an escape into the stunning winter world that others can never know. Skiing is a means of further winter activities. It is also inexpensive, available, and very, very good for your body. Finally, it provides a good opportunity to savor a rare and gravely endangered commodity—silence.

Best of all, perhaps, it's a rewarding sport for anyone who lives or travels in country where snow piles deep in winter.

CHAPTER 1

EQUIPMENT

A significant factor of cross-country skiing is that a comparatively small amount of gear is necessary to enjoy it—or even to become an expert. An average angler, for example, might make several times the investment in fishing tackle for one trip. A good set of golf clubs would cost much more, not to mention the growing cost of club and greens fees. Even downhill skiing is significantly more expensive than ski touring.

Any cross-country skier will need the following essentials and nothing more: skis, boots or shoes, bindings, poles, a waxing kit, and either a waist band carrier or a light day rucksack for carrying small items. A ski tourer may also want to buy a suit of clothing, but, as we'll see later, it isn't really necessary. Nor shall we consider camping or ski-backpacking gear as essential right here.

SKIS

It may seem surprising in this age of plastics and polyesters that as recently as 1974 three out of every four pairs of cross-country skis were made of that miracle ingredient wood—laminated wood: laminated hickory, ash, beech, and fir, to be exact. The consensus among experts and professionals is that a top touring ski should have a hickory sole with lignastone edges. Lignastone is wood compressed to metal hardness in phenolic resin.

All at once things are changing. Newer and tougher Fiberglas skis are coming on strongly and in time will surely capture most of the market. Until 1975, which can be considered a turning point, synthetic skis were more expensive than wood models. But as the sources of the proper woods (all in North America) gradually dry up, the Fiberglas skis become more and more competitive in price. Most are also more durable.

Except for the subject of waxing skis, which will be considered in Chapter 3, nothing about cross-country skiing has been made so bewildering as the proper selection of skis. It might seem to many a beginner that the aim is to discourage rather than encourage him or her right at the start. Some of the literature on the subject is baffling enough to bewilder a council of great technologists. That is most unfortunate, because it need not be.

At a busy mountain sports shop in the West, several customers of varying athletic backgrounds were allowed—even encouraged—to try out all the cross-country skis in the place that were of their proper size. Some of the customers were skiing neophytes; others had past experience. Few could detect much if any difference in the skis from lowest to highest price, whether wood laminates or synthetics. They could ski and have fun on them all, a most revealing conclusion.

Obviously, a person who is on skis for long hours day in and day out, or who is in some sort of competition, can nitpick over the fine points of one ski against another. But let's try to keep this as simple as possible for the nonpros. Let's try not to confuse anybody.

A ski of proper length for you should extend

These pictures show how to select proper length of ski and ski pole for any individual. But after some experience, individuals may find shorter—or longer —equipment more to their liking. ERWIN A. BAUER.

from the floor to your palm with arm vertically upraised. (Accompanying is a chart of both ski and pole lengths for persons of various heights.) This length allows the skis to plane well on powder and provides the contact area necessary when touring. A ski should not rest absolutely flat on a flat surface, but should have a camber (or long arch) in the center. When you stand with full weight on the ski, the camber disappears and the ski becomes flat. This feature is necessary to achieve the smooth glide forward.

Height	Ski Length	Pole Length
152 cm (5′)	180 cm	120 cm
157 cm (5′2″)	185 cm	120–125 cm
162 cm (5′4″)	190 cm	125 cm
167 cm (5′6″)	195 cm	130–135 cm
173 cm (5′8″)	200 cm	135 cm
178 cm (5′10″)	205 cm	140 cm
183 cm (6′)	210 cm	145 cm
188 cm (6′2″)	215 cm	150 cm
193 cm (6′4″)	215–220 cm	155 cm

One good way to buy skis is to have an experienced skier help you; better still if he can help you try out several different pairs. Some shops will permit this; some will not. Many shops will rent out different skis for such experimenting and then will deduct the rental paid from the purchase price of the new pair finally selected.

Written advice cannot possibly help a beginner as much as actually trying out what is best for him, for people differ far too much in physical ability, balance, and condition. There is also the matter of what type of skiing they will eventually do, how frequently, and in what kind of country. Keep in mind, also, that not all salespeople in ski shops are qualified to be advisers on cross-country gear. Far from it.

Nordic or cross-country skis have been divided into three categories. Let's refer to them as (1) general (or standard) touring, (2) light touring, and (3) racing. They differ in width, weight, type of boots, and bindings. General and light touring skis account for more than 95 per cent of all skis in use in North America.

General touring skis are the heaviest, have the greatest surface underfoot, and are the toughest. They measure about sixty millimeters wide at the binding point and weigh up to six or seven pounds a pair. For most beginners with only modest co-ordination and average balance, these are the best bets. They are found in largest supply in ski rental shops because they are best suited to once-in-a-while skiers. On the other hand, the wide standards are also preferred by veteran winter backpackers and mountaineers who have to lug heavy loads. You will also find most wilderness explorers far from established trails wearing the standard skis because others are more frail and the risk of breakage must be eliminated. Touring boots, like summertime hiking boots, are high cut above the ankle. Bindings are steel or aluminum toe pieces (more on these later), some also with heel cables or straps for heavy usage.

As skill and confidence are gained, more and more skiers, may trade in standard skis for light touring skis. Even beginners with considerable athletic background might buy them in the beginning. Averaging fifty-two millimeters wide and weighing about four pounds, these are faster and to be preferred by persons of good co-ordination and balance for touring in fairly open, level to rolling country. Light touring boots are usually

The whole difference between cross-country and downhill skiing is illustrated here. Cross-country touring boot is fastened to ski *only* by standard toe binding. Heel is free to move up and down in stride. Canvas gaiter keeps snow from overflowing into boot. ERWIN A. BAUER.

cut at the ankle and bound onto the ski with aluminum alloy toe plates.

Racing skis, which are the lightest of the three, are not widely available because of the small demand for them. These measure less than fifty millimeters wide at the bindings, may weigh less than three pounds, and must be considered very fragile when worn by anyone but a perfectly balanced racer. Low-cut footgear similar to track shoes are bound onto the thin skis with lightweight aluminum toe clamps. Design is aimed at keeping as much weight and bulk as possible off the racer's two feet.

Some other factors should be considered when first matching up a pair of skis to your own size, physique, and personal needs as well as to snow situations you will expect. Maintenance of skis is a factor, too.

For the most satisfying performance on almost all skis, it is necessary to wax the soles—bottoms —and there exist various waxes for all different snow conditions. In a single trip, it may be necessary to wax, rewax, or change waxes frequently as the snow surface changes. For some skiers this is nothing at all, if not actually a pleasant change of pace. But, depending on one's temperament, it can be a dreadful nuisance and a bore. Therefore, keep in mind that wood soles at times work well with little waxing and possibly (under ideal conditions) none at all. On the other hand, Fiberglas bases must be kept properly waxed always.

Then there is another possibility. Among the newest skis developed (and still in testing stages) are those (Trak) with "fish scale" soles, thin mohair strips or other undersurfaces that never (or so the manufacturers claim) require wax. Most sophisticated skiers and (I've noticed) salespeople who are trying to seem sophisticated, scoff at these. But no-wax skis just aren't bad. Peggy and I have tested them extensively and find them more than satisfactory, except under conditions of the wettest (or rapidly melting) snows. We recommend them to any who are badly bugged by the chore of waxing.

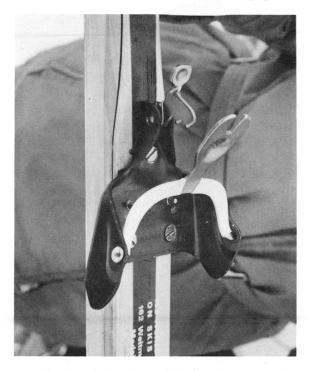

Toe binding of plastic for light touring and racing. ERWIN A. BAUER.

BOOTS AND BINDINGS

Footwear for cross-country skiers comes in synthetic material and in leather, with either synthetic or leather soles, below and above the ankle in height, either lined or unlined with fur or synthetic pile. Which to buy is again a matter of personal preference, and it is wise to try out different boots in the field before purchasing, if possible. One advantage of synthetics is that they remain waterproof after long, tough use, but they cannot be sewn or repaired as leather can. All synthetic boot material is poor insulation and should be lined, except possibly in racing models.

Care should be taken to buy boots that fit well. That means they should fit snugly all over, but they shouldn't be tight. One exception to the snugness might be in the toe, where I (and most others) like to have a little extra space. The same thickness of socks should be worn whenever you are trying out new boots, just as when you are actually out skiing. Leather boots should be well broken in before you use them on any long ski tours. One way to accomplish this quickly is to wear them all the time around the house.

A perfect boot binding is one that allows the same flexibility, freedom, and comfort as when you are wearing a favorite old pair of hiking

The light touring binding is both fastened and unfastened with the point of the ski pole. Bending over to do it isn't necessary. ERWIN A. BAUER.

Overall view of how light touring, low-cut boots fit onto skis. ERWIN A. BAUER.

shoes—or even canvas sneakers. Bindings should be installed free on the skis by whoever sells them. Today the cut of the toe of all boot soles is *squarish and standardized,* to fit exactly into any ski bindings. In other words, all boots and bindings now fit together; any pair of ski shoes should fit into any bindings, no matter where the two were separately manufactured.

The connection between boot and ski is made by three small pegs on the bindings; three equally spaced holes in the boot soles fit down over these, and the sole is clamped in that position. The actual clamping is done by thumb pressure or, on some, by pushing down with the point of the ski pole. The ski poles are handy for removing the skis after sprawling awkwardly in a snow drift. Some bindings can be slightly adjusted for freer or tighter clamping, the latter for wilderness or steep-country touring. A solidly secure binding, if properly installed, should not twist off easily or come unclamped at every sudden turn in the trail or every shift in the skier's balance.

In addition to the three-peg toe clamp, some cross-country ski tourers carrying heavy loads on their backs for venturing far in rough country will prefer a cable binding around the back of the heel. That is mostly for added insurance against losing the ski in a tough spot. Another kind of leather or neoprene binding similar to those used with snowshoes, with a strap around the heel, is available in some places. This makes it possible to ski on any kind of hunting boot or pac, rather than on the standardized skiing boots. We have tried these on a couple of occasions and, except

for use in certain emergencies, do not recommend them at all.

Keep in mind that the main difference between cross-country and downhill skiing is all right there—*in the binding.* When he is hurtling downhill, the skier is affixed flat-footed—heel and toe onto his skis. But the ski tourer is fastened only at the toe, an arrangement that gives him vastly more freedom and mobility.

SKI POLES

Cross-country skiers require two poles, which may be made of bamboo, Fiberglas, or metal. The latter two are preferred and also are the most expensive. Select poles of the proper length by standing erect, feet together, and with one arm stretched straight out from the body. The pole should measure as far as the distance from the ground to a point between your elbow and armpit. The ski length chart (page 9) also shows approximate ski-pole lengths for skiers of different heights. All poles should have adjustable handstraps.

The ideal poles should be strong but light and springy, because they will certainly be used to help propel you over the snow as well as to maintain balance at times. Bamboo poles might split axially under heaviest use, but all but the worst splits can be repaired by wrapping the poles with stout tape. I've seen a good many alpine or downhill poles in use by ski tourers, but these are a false economy, because they are unnecessarily heavy and are not designed to flex as are Nordic poles. Besides, the best cross-country poles are not very expensive.

All poles have circular webbed baskets about 5 or 6 inches above the pointed metal tips. Baskets come in different diameters, but few skiers are likely to interchange baskets or to own more than one pair of all purpose poles. Baskets of 4½ to 5 inches in diameter are most suitable for average snow conditions. In either wet (rapidly melting) snow or fresh soft powder, a larger-diameter basket can give a skier a better "grip."

Check out the straps on poles you contemplate buying. Be sure they can be quickly adjusted (and with cold fingers) to fit when you are wearing light gloves or, on warm days, no gloves, as well as when changing to heavy mittens on the coldest days.

WAXING KIT

Waxing skis properly is complicated enough to be considered in a separate chapter. But unless a ski tourer opts for the no-wax skis described before, a waxing kit will be absolutely essential. A kit will contain a selection of waxes to cope with all snow conditions, and we will cover these in the waxing discussion. The kit will also include a large hand-size cork for spreading and applying wax, as well as a metal scraper for removing it. To save time and elbow grease, some skiers like to have a small propane torch, which heats wax for easier application and later for scraping it off. On all tours except very short local runs, most skiers like to carry along their wax kits, excepting the torch.

CARRYING DEVICES

There are two options here, the waist pack carrier and the rucksack. The best is the one that "wears" most comfortably on your body—or that has the proper capacity. Many downhill skiers and day hikers have long ago become used to waist packs. So why change? The packs can carry waxes, snacks, a compass, a folded-up windbreaker and other small items. But since I never go ski touring without taking a camera, extra lenses, and film, plus other items, I prefer a light, compartmented nylon rucksack. When it is full of photo gear at the beginning of the snow season, the straps do bite into my shoulders. But after a week or so, I hardly notice that the weight is there.

Incidentally, carrying a camera (especially with a heavy lens) around the neck in rough or hilly country isn't wise. It's too easy to dunk the outfit

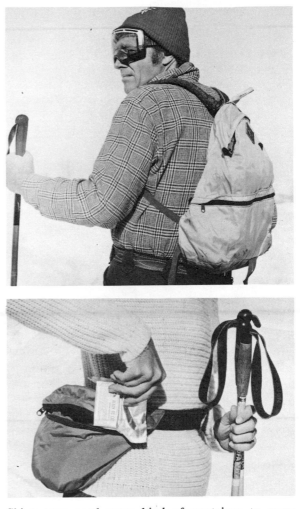

Ski tourers need some kind of container to carry lunch, spare tips, camera, and other necessities. The choice is between a light rucksack (or day pack) and a belt pack. ERWIN A. BAUER.

in wet snow, and the strap can act as a choker in case of a sudden spill. It is better to carry the works in a rucksack and take it out only when you are ready to shoot.

There, from skis to wax and carrying pack, is all that anyone needs to start out on cross-country skiing. At the beginning of the 1977 season a complete outfit good for many years of hard, steady use could be purchased for under $100. About $150 would cover the most expensive basic set of ski running gear. But of course these prices cannot be expected to hold in a steadily inflating market. The good news is that ski touring will still be less expensive than most other sports, while it offers much greater rewards.

CHAPTER 2

CROSS-COUNTRY CLOTHING

The whole point of cross-country skiing is enjoyment. There is no need to impress anyone with elegant plumage, and there is no required uniform—which leaves the tourer free of current fashion's tyranny or any other need to conform. Forget about the "right color" for this season and the *"in* ski look." Instead, consider that you may already own all the cross-country skiing togs you need. If what you have meets two requirements, it's more than acceptable.

First, you must keep dry and warm—always. Second, your clothing must allow maximum unrestricted movement of your body. The skier who becomes overly damp and chilled, or who can't move arms and legs easily, will be a victim too soon of discomfort and fatigue. Therefore, while no particular garments are required, there are general items of clothing that need to be considered here.

Most outdoorsmen who venture afield and are active during cold weather know about the layers principle. This is a way to keep warm by adding or subtracting fairly light garments—layers, really—as body temperature changes, rather than by wearing a single heavy garment. Starting out on a cold morning, to illustrate, a person will wear several layers of clothing. As he warms up, he will remove layers so as to retain body heat but at the same time not to overheat. As evening approaches and the temperature falls, he can put the clothing layers back on again as they are needed. This is the gospel for cross-country skiing and skiers. So let's start with the first layer and work outward.

UNDERWEAR

When it is really warm and still (as it may often be at the tag end of the skiing season) and you are not skiing far enough to worry about weather changes, you may not need long underwear. Wear what you would normally wear on an Indian summer hike, which might be a suit of very light cotton or net longjohns. But skip the nylon or synthetic fibers, which are not as absorbent as cotton and do not "give" to exercise as well.

But with more normal winter temperatures and the chance of high winds, more protection is necessary, and that means long underwear. You have a choice of one- and two-piece; of cotton, wool, quilted thermal, or many combinations of all these. Whether you like your longhandles in two parts or one depends upon your preference and what material you can tolerate against bare, goose-pimpled skin. But when the tops of evergreen trees are whipping in the wild wind and pellets of snow are flying, Peggy and I have long depended upon a certain kind of one-piecer available from Eddie Bauer Outfitters in Seattle. Other outfitters offer similar underwear.

Admittedly they are expensive, but these longjohns have also been long-serving. Made of 20 per cent angora rabbit, 45 per cent wool, and 35 per cent acrylic, they breathe, bend without stretching, wash well, and never leave a cold gap open around the midsection, as do two-piecers. Zippers that run the full length in front and that provide a drop seat in the rear have not yet given

Members of a ski-touring party may wear different kinds of clothing, but still they will all be comfortable. ERWIN A. BAUER.

any problems. Short cotton knit pants worn underneath our one-piecers extend the time between laundering.

A lot of lady skiers go braless. This is a luxurious freedom. Under layers of clothing, no one will notice, even if you or anyone should care. Besides, female comfort will soar.

SOCKS

No one can travel very far and enjoy it, either on or off skis, unless his feet are warm and comfortable. Any foot traveler's feet must also be dry, which means wearing proper and correctly fitted socks. We always wear two pairs, believing there is sound reason for it.

The inner pair is of the same thick woolen material that we use when hiking, hunting, or backpacking before the first snow falls. They are of rough gray "unfinished" wool and are usually sold as "Norwegian ski socks" or something similar. The outer pair (frequently trade-named "insulation socks") is of the thick wicking type which, theoretically, permits perspiration to move

upward and out of the boot. Up to a point it seems to work. Or maybe it's just that I like the comfortable cushion that the two-sock thickness provides. But the main thing, one pair or two, is to wear fairly new, fresh socks (without holes or any roughly patched-up heels) that fit. Cheap socks that do not fit, that stretch when damp, that come loose and form folds inside shoes can cause terrible irritation and blisters. So wear whatever socks you like, but take my advice and do not skimp on quality. On more ambitious trips, change to dry socks as frequently as possible. Wash socks often, because the cleaner they are, the more moisture they can absorb.

SHIRTS

For milder days a good choice is a cotton knit shirt with a long tail and with or without a turtle neck. This will be moderately absorbent and not too warm. But if it's colder, make that a wool shirt. The qualities of wool are well known to outdoorsmen, it is being warm even when damp, and very, very durable. A 100 per cent wool shirt will be excellent, but a large part of those available on sporting goods shelves will be part wool and part synthetic fiber blend.

The same style of shirt used for hunting, fishing, and other kinds of outdoor work will be as good as any for ski touring. It helps if they have long tails and are fully buttoned all the way down the front. But anyone who wants to be fancy—or colorful—might want to invest in one of the woolen sweaters used by downhill skiers. They're good, too.

PANTS

No doubt because the "costume" originated in Europe, where styles are supposed to be more chic, the tradition of wearing knickers when you are cross-country skiing still survives in the United States and Canada. At least one still sees knickers being worn in the East, although not so many west of the Mississippi. Still, there is good reason for it: The knicker design allows near-maximum movement of the legs, plus comfort. Whether you wear knickers or not may depend on whether you tend toward the traditional or not and whether you want to fork over the extra money for a pair. If you're female and happen to have a lithe, slim figure, it's one man's opinion that you'll look a lot better skiing in western jeans.

For not-too-bitter days, jeans or any loose-fitting trousers are just fine for a typical day-long ski run. Naturally, they should be large enough to fit over whatever longjohns you're wearing and still not restrict your movements. That means well-worn, oft-laundered jeans rather than stiff, new, tight ones. We've seen many (maybe most) skiers wearing any old roomy woolen trousers or slacks, and that casual attire didn't adversely affect performance. Pants to avoid are very baggy ones or those with wide flares, which can catch onto brush or snags in passing. The bottoms of some pants can be tucked into the tops of socks and held there with a rubber band or covered with gaiters, about which more later.

Summed up: Wear the pants (or anything) that feel good and comfortable. If you worry too much about how they look, you may have taken the wrong trail.

Complete freedom of movement and comfort—the ability to strike out unencumbered—are far more important than style and chic in cross-country skiing apparel. NEW HAMPSHIRE OFFICE OF VACATION TRAVEL. PHOTO BY DICK SMITH.

MORE LAYERS

Now you need another layer (in extreme cold, maybe two layers) to go over your upper body, and there are a number of good options. One would be a sweater. Let's start by advising you to leave at home the numerous acrylics and synthetics that are available. Instead, choose a 100 per cent loose-knit wool, a pullover rather than a cardigan. The finest woolen sweaters are those that are unprocessed and untreated, to retain most of the natural lanolin. They usually have a rough and genuine outdoor look rather than a smooth, fashionable appearance. Rain, snow, or beads of moisture that collect on the surface of these sweaters can be brushed away, and body moisture will evaporate through it without saturating the garment. In other words, these sweaters are ideal.

But so are vests. More and more we see these worn instead of sweaters. Some are of sheepskin with the wool turned inside, and some are of quilted goose down or Dacron. All were first worn by western ranchers and were adopted by big-game hunters. They serve cross-country skiers very well, too, being light in weight and very warm when fitted properly down over the kidney area. Some also have turn-up collars in the back and large, handy pockets for film and snacks. They're inferior to sweaters in that they do not provide cover for the arms. But when you are actively in motion, this becomes a plus because vests never bind and give total arm freedom to push those ski poles.

Ski tourers should own and usually carry one more upper garment. For day-long or shorter trips it can be a lightweight shell jacket, which is a windbreaker as much as anything else. Made of cotton poplin or a tight-weave cotton-synthetic or nylon, these are not meant to be worn when you are moving. Instead they should be slipped on during rest stops or at the end of a tour to hold the warm air close to your body and to deflect cold winds. This garment should be light enough to be stuffed into your carrying pack or perhaps tied around your waist by the sleeves.

For longer tours or for backpacking or camping trips, a skier needs something heavier than just a light windbreaker. The choice here is for the best and lightest (in weight) goose down or Dacron coat, with parka hood attached or attachable, that you can afford. This might well be the same jacket you have used for deer hunting, hockey watching, or ice fishing, but again it is to be worn after a run rather than during the skiing. Whenever I take along this kind of jacket, I do so by lashing it onto my rucksack. It is a great garment to slip into when you are unwinding or thoroughly fatigued after a long, hard cross-country trip. In a ski camp you can either wear it to sleep or use it as a pillow.

Warm-up pants of the type used by downhill skiers can also be a comfort at the end of a day. But they are certainly not to be worn when you are actually skiing, because of the heat and sweat that will be trapped inside. If you already own

Most ski tourers wisely use the layer system: several garments (here shirt, vest, and windbreaker jacket) that can be removed or added as the weather and the skiing require. ERWIN A. BAUER.

them, or something similar, it doesn't hurt to carry warm-up pants in your car for bundling up en route home.

Most cross-country skiers need a pair of gaiters. These really are leggings meant to cover up the top of the skier's boot so that deep snow doesn't get inside to soak socks and feet. There are high gaiters that reach above the calf and low ones that resemble the gentleman's spats commonly worn during the early part of this century. Fashioned of duck or similar waterproof fabric, some are laced and some are zippered along one side, then secured under the boot sole and at the top with drawstrings.

It's not an infallible rule of ski-touring fashion, but most skiers who wear knickers also wear the low or ankle-high gaiters. Skiers in jeans or trousers wear the calf-high gaiters and tuck the pants inside them. Although they are available everywhere, gaiters are easy to custom-make on home sewing machines from scrap tenting cloth. We have seen some very colorful ones with bright patterns sewn or painted—even embroidered—on the sides. If zippers are used, stick to nylon instead of metal, which rusts and seems to freeze up much more easily.

Any gaiter should be made to cover up completely the lacings of the ski boots and, thereby, make them easy to untie at the end of a run. That is immensely important when fingers are nearly numb, the sun is sinking fast, and a raw wind is whistling.

HEADGEAR

When you are completely dressed and exercising normally, more heat is dissipated from the head than from any other single part of the body. The frost you often see collected on a skier's cap, hair, and beard is visible evidence of the great amount of moisture plus heat that is escaping from around the head. A hat, then, is extremely important in regulating the proper body temperature. Hat on, ears covered, and you're warm —perhaps even too warm. Head uncovered and you soon cool off—perhaps too cool and too soon.

The tuque, which is probably of Canadian origin, has become the traditional headgear of many cross-country skiers. But probably no greater variety of winter caps can be observed anywhere than along a busy ski trail. Most are colorful and actually exude the pure, unconfined joy of the sport. But back to the tuque (pronounced tyook), which is really a loosely knitted cap with a tassel on top. Tassels and pompoms add nothing except jauntiness to the cap and may even catch onto low trees branches in woodland passing, but I like them.

Again, wool is the preferred material for a cap, which you should be able to pull down over the ears or roll up above them. Some skiers have less tolerance to cold ears than others, and they solve the problem by wearing a headband (or earband) either with or without a cap. Frostbitten ears are no joke, particularly since it is impossible to wiggle them like frostbitten toes. Bright reds, oranges, or greens in caps or headbands

Peggy Bauer shows what the fashionable ski tourer would probably wear—bulky knit ski sweater, knickers, knee socks, and crocheted floppy-brim cap. ERWIN A. BAUER.

A knit cap that can be pulled down over the ears is more or less standard—and jaunty—on ski trails. ERWIN A. BAUER.

Besides usual layers, and especially when camping out, the skier should have a warm fur-lined or down-filled outer jacket and warm mittens. ERWIN A. BAUER.

make them easier to spot from a distance, a fact that could be important one day.

A warm cap is really a lightweight thermostat. If a skier feels he's getting too warm, he can remove it, hoping to prevent perspiration from accumulating toward future chill. Of course, the opposite is true. A hatless skier can fend off an oncoming chill by putting on a cap. He can even warm up feet and hands, our best medical advisers assure us, by covering up an uncovered head.

GLOVES

Probably because I handle metal cameras and lenses more than most, by necessity with bare hands, that is where I suffer first and most se-

verely from cold. So do some others, and, for them, gloves are even more vital for cross-country skiing. Hands, like all the rest of the human body, warm up with physical exertion. But being farthest out, at the end of the "heat line," fingers warm up most slowly and cool off first when left uncovered. Hands, like heads, should be covered and uncovered as often as conditions and cold demand.

A skier can wear gloves or mittens. Mittens are warmer than gloves of the same material. Mittens with leather palms on a knitted body—better still, all leather with foam, Dacron, or fur lining—are great favorites when it's really cold and windy. But there is plenty to be said for a pair of wool knit gloves or mittens inside a waterproof and windproof outer shell when weather is likely to fluctuate greatly. On the other hand, soft, supple gloves may be all that is necessary for comfort during a brisk tour across a sunshiny landscape.

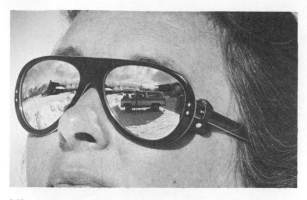

Mirror lenses are coated, have high density, and are suitable protection against snow glare. ERWIN A. BAUER.

EYE PROTECTION

Early in this chapter, I pointed out that no specific gear is necessary for cross-country skiing and that a wide variety of garments you already own are adaptable. The same is mostly true of sunglasses. On all but the dullest days you are going to need something to shield the eyes from great glare, and possibly you already own the lenses to do it. But if not, read on.

Consider first what is *not* recommended: small lenses and bluish or pinkish tints in any size. The smaller the lenses, the more glare reaches the eye from around the edges. Also, an eye is drawn to the contrast line around the lens edges, and it becomes harder for a skier to concentrate on the trail and terrain before him. Gray, gray-green, or green-tinted lenses are best, for these shades do not upset the natural color balance and so do not greatly change the winter picture you see. Amber or yellow is recommended for overcast days, for they enable a wearer to spot humps, dips, and moguls in the snow and so avoid spilling over them.

Photochromic glasses that darken in a bright sun and lighten up in dull light are satisfactory except perhaps on the most dazzling bright days over snow. It is probably wisest to consult your ophthalmologist before relying on them. Be aware also that these photochromics darken only in the presence of direct ultraviolet rays that are blocked by glass. Before investing in them, be advised that they do not work when you are driving in a car or looking through the windshield of a boat or plane.

This skier wears a wool knit cap that can be pulled down to cover the ears, a woolen hunting shirt, a day pack (or rucksack) to carry gear, and ventilated, wrap-around glasses. ERWIN A. BAUER.

Good glasses with gray or gray-green tints and large lenses are essential when you are touring over bright landscapes. ERWIN A. BAUER.

Most prescription sunglasses are fine, because the lenses are large. Bifocals can be troublesome in that, when you are looking down close and directly ahead, the ground will be blurred. A solution is to have prescription glasses made with only your long-distance prescription, because when you are skiing there is no need to read fine print.

Polaroid glasses will do no harm—or little good—because they block glare from only one angle. Contact lenses are fine and should be worn in place. But since they probably make you even more sensitive to light than nonwearers are, wear a pair of deep-gray-tinted nonprescription glasses over them. But a good many cross-country skiers find that no eyeglasses at all are really suitable, and for them the answer is often a pair of plastic goggles of the type developed for downhill skiing and snowmobiling. They do have a number of advantages, if they are ventilated around the edges.

Goggles fit well and more securely than glasses. Plastic permits less ultraviolet to penetrate to the eyes than glass. Plastic is tougher and can stand more abuse. But goggles should fit snugly around the sides, should be tinted yellow or amber, and should be flat-surfaced all across the front to pre-vent distortion. The only problem is that nobody has yet been able to keep goggles from fogging up. There isn't any choice except to pause at intervals to wipe them off, which isn't so bad after all.

OTHER ITEMS

This is entirely personal, but I consider a dickey to be worth its weight in comfort. It is just a detached turtleneck with brief chest- and back-piece that can be slipped on or off in a second, under any shirt or jacket. For me it is better than a turtleneck shirt, because it can be used to hold heat (when a person stops exercising) or removed to allow cooling. My dickey is also a concession to luxury in that it is cashmere wool. But it weighs only a few ounces and takes almost no space inside my rucksack.

Being properly clad for skiing will prevent everything from frostbite to snow blindness in the extremes. But it will also make any day on the trail more happy and comfortable.

CHAPTER 3

PREPARING TO SKI

To perform in any sport reasonably well—and to enjoy performing—it is necessary to prepare or train for it properly. That includes physical conditioning and getting the equipment in shape to use. Cross-country skiing is no exception; a skier must pay some attention to his body and to his skis.

PHYSICAL CONDITIONING

The time to start training for the snow season and ski touring, if possible, is well before the first snow falls. But the training does not have to be an ordeal or even the least bit unpleasant. For many it may simply mean being active every day —or at least *more* active—than is the normal routine. But that advice is good for anyone, no matter whether he plans to ski tour or not.

The most basic training can consist of just walking to work every day, for at least part of the distance, instead of riding. Or bicycling. Develop leg muscles for skiing by walking up steps everywhere, even daily to the tenth floor at the office, instead of relying on elevators. Other ways to get in shape include swimming, jogging, or playing handball or tennis, if you happen to be citybound and limited recreational facilities are available. No matter what the conditioning or where, the emphasis should be on frequency. Exercise often, regularly, and in some moderation, rather than infrequently and strenuously. Manage some kind of workout every day.

It isn't advisable to begin serious and vigorous cross-country skiing suddenly, without preparing for it. That is doubly true for persons beyond forty, say who have long lived a sedentary life, who have been overweight for some time, who are heavy drinkers or smokers, or who suffer from potential or latent heart conditions. Some survivors of heart attacks can and do go ski touring, but they do it in moderation and with a doctor monitoring the activity. Skiing is a wonderfully complete physical conditioner itself, but the emphasis must be on moderation, on getting into it slowly.

Nowadays cardiologists can detect heart irregularities by EKG tests (which skiers past forty should have), and they can recommend whether one should ski or not. But given sound hearts, even out-of-condition people can begin to get in shape by walking regularly. It's best to do this on a fixed program from six to twelve weeks before a skiing holiday.

Every day for the first week, walk one mile in twenty minutes, or more if that seems too easy. Swing your arms and flex your muscles, breathing deeply as you do so. Keep increasing the distance daily until you are covering two miles in thirty minutes or faster, which is a pace almost anybody should be able to attain in a month of hiking. If that seems too easy, jog part of the way. Or add training weights to your shoes. Add pushups and situps to the daily regimen. Another way to increase the physical effort gradually is to switch from sidewalks or level trails to hillier and steeper places. Bicycling will test leg muscles even more.

The author illustrates one excellent way for city-bound skiers to get in shape—climbing seats repeatedly at a local stadium or sports arena. It develops legs and lungs. ERWIN A. BAUER.

If you happen to be locked up inside a city, seek out the nearest athletic stadium or running track and work out there. Try climbing up and down empty bleacher seats, increasing the number of climbs every day. Another excellent way to strengthen the leg muscles is to walk up steps (or bleacher seats) backward. It really is possible to put on skis for the first time and, except for learning the basics, to compete in stamina with almost any instructor.

Many beginners discover that arms tire more quickly than legs; this is understandable, because arms, in modern living, are even more neglected than legs. Arms may furnish up to a quarter of a ski tourer's propulsion, and so the upper body should also be given attention when you are getting ready to hit the trails.

Training skis mounted on ball-bearing-roller wheels are available (from Silva of Indiana, for one) for anyone serious enough to want to practice the cross-country glide on dry ground. Ski racers, especially, use training aids during the off-season. But lacking the roller skis, a great way to condition the chest and arms is to walk directly up steep hills while using the ski poles exactly as in skiing to help push ahead. Start this slowly and increase it as your strength grows. For any who feel foolish doing this in shorts, with autumn's leaves littering the ground, we recommend retreating to a basement or gym to work out the arms with a medicine ball or elastic stretch bands. According to many female skiers, this accomplishes far more than just getting the arms in shape for pushing ski poles.

KNOW BASIC FIRST AID

More because of the cold environment, perhaps, than the chance of serious injury, cross-country skiers should know at least basic first aid before venturing very far. This is rarely a part of skiing instruction, but we consider it important anyway. Besides, first-aid courses are sponsored in many places, usually free, by the local chapter of the Red Cross, community fire and police departments, Boy and Girl Scouts, state fish and game departments, YMCAs, and adult education centers. Also you can attend one of the two- or three-day refresher courses in first aid offered by the ski rescue patrols at many downhill skiing centers.

Most cross-country skiing emergencies are likely to be no more than simple frostbite. Fortunately, frostbite is easily prevented and is easy to cope with after a small amount of instruction. Feet and fingers—the extremities—always get cold first. But try not to let them get cold in the first place. A good way to warm fingers is to don whatever shirt, jacket, or cap is not being worn and then to swing the arms vigorously in full circles. Just a little of this should restore circulation and soon warm fingers all the way out to the tips.

Cold toes are a little harder to cope with. If wiggling them inside the boots and traveling at a more rapid pace doesn't work, loosen the boot laces slightly to try to restore some circulation. Jump or stamp in place, laces loose. If all that fails, stop long enough to build a small fire over which to apply heat gradually (never quickly) to the cold parts. At the same time, rub your toes gently. When they are warm again, get moving as soon as possible, trying to hold a smooth, heat-maintaining pace, which we shall discuss later.

Despite warming efforts, frostbite still might occur. If your skin turns very pale and glassy, assume that frostbite is developing. Without treatment it will turn white, waxy, and firm to the touch. Treat it immediately by covering it and warming it; never rub the frostbitten tissue, because you might break the skin. Never apply snow or cold water (often advised, incorrectly, in the past). Instead, apply water only slightly warmer than body temperature.

Here is a very important thing to remember. A skier can travel a short distance on thoroughly frostbitten—frozen—feet or toes, but it is terribly dangerous to do so, and after the feet or toes have thawed, the frostbitten areas become extremely painful. The person should then be carried.

Basic first-aid training will help to solve other problems—foreign objects in the eye, slight sprains, cuts, and bruises—which are bound to occur. But mostly it will save valuable time on the trail, which might otherwise be lost.

GETTING EQUIPMENT READY FOR SKIING

In the entire subject of cross-country skiing, nothing is more difficult to discuss than the most important matter of waxing skis. With the exception of skis that do not require wax (noted in Chapter 1), waxing is necessary to obtain maximum ease of skiing and greatest enjoyment of the sport. It improves technique and is as important as sharpening ice skates, dressing a flyline, or lubricating a bicycle. It is vastly more complicated than any of these, however, being without question the greatest nuisance any cross-country skier will ever have to confront.

The reason for waxing is to prepare a pair of skis so that the tourer can glide effortlessly on the flat or downhill, but at the same time be able to climb up at least moderate hills without sliding backward. The wax both grips and glides, a characteristic that at first would seem impossible.

Every snow surface has microscopic irregulari-ties—a rough surface that the unaided human eye cannot see. As a waxed ski glides over this surface, imperceptibly the snow crystals melt and form a friction-free glaze. But when the same waxed ski comes down hard on the snow for that brief instant in which the skier kicks—thrusts forward—that same microscopically irregular surface grips the wax and keeps the ski from slipping backward. To slip backward with every kick, even extremely slightly, can turn skiing into hard, unpleasant work.

It has often been written that with a good (or perfect) wax job, touring skis that have the best glide also have the best grip. That is pure bunk. No matter how you do it, either glide or grip is sacrificed, and it is best to sacrifice some glide in favor of a good grip.

A revealing incident comes to mind whenever waxing is discussed. Three veteran, capable cross-country instructors were leading groups of skiers on a short tour in the same area. All three estimated the air temperature (as is proper), judged the quality of the snow surface (also standard operating procedure), and then advised the students how to wax skis to suit the conditions. The advice of all three experts was totally different. And the students in one group averaged about as well on the snow as those in the other groups.

Proceeding on that basis, here is how we advise waxing skis. First, decide on one commercial brand or system of waxes and waxing—and stick with it for a while. A list of the most popular and most available would include Swix, Skilom, Bass, Bratlie, Fall-Line, Holmenkol, Ostbye, Toko, Ride, Rex, Vauhti, Ex-Elit, Johannsen, and, no doubt, many newer entries on the market. Each one of these includes a selection of waxes, one or more applicators, and instructions on how to use them. The beginner is advised to follow the instructions exactly—to the letter—until through experience and association with other skiers he finds some better combination. If you do a lot of skiing, you will have plenty of time to experiment. But trying to provide some kind of "handy cross-country waxing guide" here in print—one that covers the use of all waxes in general —would be useless.

We can, however, discuss some general facts and principles about waxing. Waxes come in cans, metal-foil cylinders, tubes (as for tooth-

Most skis must be given first a base wax, and then a wax to suit the day's snow conditions. Waxing can be a nuisance and time-consuming. ERWIN A. BAUER.

Skis are usually carried in cartop carriers. But before use it will be necessary to clean road dirt off bottoms after a long trip. ERWIN A. BAUER.

Typical ski wax kit contains several tubes of different waxes, some exceedingly sticky, plus a scraper and a cork applicator/spreader. ERWIN A. BAUER.

A new development is that wax can be removed (for rewaxing) with push-button spray can remover. Without this it's a sticky chore. ERWIN A. BAUER.

paste), and spray-on cans. The number of different types, usually color-keyed for quick use and identification by the manufacturers, must run far into the hundreds and is bewildering to experts, let alone beginners. In general, however, there are the hard waxes for dryer, newly fallen, or settled snow, and for the coldest temperatures. Softer waxes are for newer snow that is wetter and for warmer temperatures. Klister waxes are for still wetter snow and slush conditions and often are right for the tag end of the skiing season. The harder the waxes, the easier and less messy they are to apply. Klisters, on the other hand, are among the stickiest substances known to man, and application is very tedious. You should do it carefully enough to confine the klister to ski bottoms alone.

Although not always possible, it is best to wax skis indoors, because the wax is easier to apply, spread, and even remove or change at room temperature. Start with a clean, dry ski, because wax will not adhere as well to a wet or dirty surface. Skis that have been carried for long distances in cartop carriers should first be scoured of road dirt (oil and grime mixed) before waxing. Incidentally, when you are on a long trip, it is well to carry skis (if they are outside the car) in plastic containers.

Most waxes are applied directly from the container. They are spread—by hand with a metal or plastic scraper or a large chunk of cork. Skis (especially wooden ones) should be given a good wax base consisting of several consecutive coats of hard wax carefully applied with even strokes and rubbed in. The finished coating should be smooth and not sticky to the touch. Waxes for various skiing conditions are applied on top of this and changed as necessary. During bright days when the weather warms or changes greatly, it is necessary to change or reapply waxes many times to maintain skiing ease. This is one of the nuisances of waxing.

If the weather is very cold, wax should be applied and rubbed with a cork applicator into a gloss. If it is warm and wet, leave the wax surface rough and unpolished. For really sloppy conditions, it may be necessary to glop on the klister and leave it that way to get any grip at all. In recent years lightweight torches that burn cartridges of butane or LP gas have been used to smooth on wax and, more important, to remove it. Even the smallest torches are too bulky to carry in the field, but they are handy to have around ski-warming bases or camps.

From all the foregoing, it is obvious that waxing is not a major joy of skiing. It is a necessary evil. Of course, the time will come, it is hoped, when the perfect ski, suitable to all situations with no need of wax, is developed. Significant steps have already been taken in that direction; the most noteworthy is the Trak ski, a Norwegian import with a fish-scale pattern over 60 per cent of the plastic bottom surface. On three out of four days afield, the Trak performs as well as the best waxed skis. It is slightly noisier, and some glide is sacrificed. But no time is lost changing and rechanging wax when days are bright, and it is wonderful to be moving on the trail.

Fortunately, no other skiing gear requires as much attention as ski bottoms. If a person is in fair physical shape and his skis have a passable wax job, he is ready to enjoy the greatest moments of any winter, of any year.

CHAPTER 4

HOW TO SKI—BASIC TO ADVANCED

Anyone who can walk briskly and steadily can ski across country. Previous athletic experience is helpful but not absolutely necessary. Traveling on skis is remarkably similar to traveling on foot. More than half of the enthusiastic cross-country skiers today have never had any training, and many of the rest have had only a few brief lessons. In the beginning, for example, I had only one hour of the most basic instruction. Cross-country skiing is a technique that anyone can pick up easily and quickly.

If there is any difficulty at all in the beginning, it can usually be blamed on the unfamiliarity of something long and large being attached to your feet. You suddenly seem to have mobility or, if the ground is slippery, you seem to have too much mobility. Without question (despite my own lack of early instruction), the best way to learn cross-country skiing correctly is to take a course in it with an expert instructor and demonstrator. Nowadays lessons for neophytes are available free (or at least very inexpensively) in many places such as adult physical education centers, high schools and universities, YMCAs, ski touring and athletic clubs, outdoor leadership and conservation schools, mountaineering and sporting goods stores, and even at many of the popular downhill skiing resorts. It's very worthwhile to check out all the possibilities where you live, because some training facilities almost certainly exist. If they do not, go out and ski anyway.

HOW TO START OUT

To begin, select a level, snow-covered area free of obstacles. It can be a park, a golf course, playing field, parking lot, or any other level real estate. Wax your skis (instructions on this in Chapter 3) and put them on. Now start walking or shuffling forward, one ski after the other. The first goal should be to get the feel of skis attached to feet.

Probably there will be no other ski tracks to follow, so make your own, packing down the snow in parallel tracks, the tracks being just about the same distance apart as when you walk. Keep walking back and forth over your own tracks and note how quickly you feel secure and gain confidence. Soon you will be ready to switch from the ski walk to what has been called the cross-country glide or motion.

Exactly as when walking, start out with the right leg forward. Just as the body weight also moves forward onto the right foot, swing the left foot forward. With body weight coming down onto the left foot, swing the right foot forward. And so on.

But right here we insert a very vital point. Do not drag the skis as you go forward; that would be as bad as dragging or shuffling your feet when you walk. Rather, lift each ski as it passes the other, from which you give a gentle thrust for-

Many expert cross-country skiers today never had a lesson. But the best way is to go out with an expert and learn techniques quickly and correctly from the very beginning. Reading about it can't match expert instruction outdoors. VAIL PHOTO BY PETER RUNYON.

The proper smooth, forward glide illustrated in a single photo. On packed snow, considerable speed is possible with minimum physical effort. This glide isn't hard for most beginners to achieve quickly. ERWIN A. BAUER.

Forward kick or glide illustrated from overhead.
ERWIN A. BAUER.

ward. At most the lifted ski should barely brush the snow surface. There is one obvious difference from walking: It is simply that when you plant either foot ahead, it doesn't stop there, as when you are walking. Instead, it glides. And the series of smooth glides becomes the almost effortless ski-touring motion or stride.

It is hard to describe in words how to start skiing properly and achieve the touring glide. But be patient and persistent, and suddenly you will achieve it. Few athletic movements ever come more easily. Beginners, once they've "caught" the stride, just want to go and go.

Still, it is sound advice (if you are not young, agile, and athletic) to proceed with caution and to ski initially in small doses. Like swimming, ski touring is a total exercise that brings muscles into play that may not otherwise be tested. There is no good in straining these muscles when gradual breaking in will do it better. Curb initial enthusiasm somewhat, and stop and rest often. Individuals who do not get outdoors frequently to hike may find that a half mile or more all at once is exhausting.

USING SKI POLES

Some ski instructors advise using ski poles right from the beginning; most instructors, perhaps, do not. Anyway, the moment the beginner starts to lengthen his stride and gain speed (compare it to changing from walking to jogging) is the time to pick up the poles and use them as part of the touring motion.

The proper technique is to begin with right leg and left arm forward, the left pole, in a firm grip, having been planted in the snow. As the left ski swings forward, the left arm is thrust backward, pushing on the pole at the end of the motion. Simultaneously the right pole is swung forward and planted in the snow just as the right ski starts to swing ahead. Correctly co-ordinating pole movements to the skiing stride gives an extra forward push, or "kick," which adds speed, almost (it seems) effortlessly. The co-ordinated leg and arm movements of a cross-country skier are beautiful to experience and to watch.

A

E

F

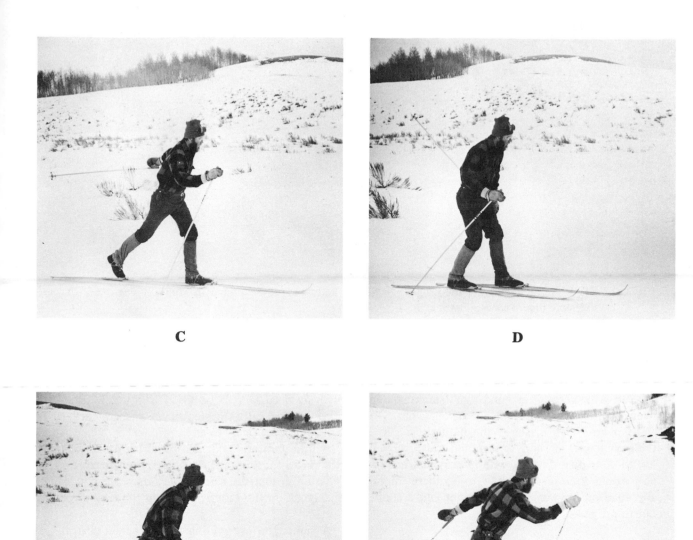

C D

G H

Basic stride as illustrated by ski-tour instructor John Crane. **A** right foot/ski has been moved forward and briefly planted as the left foot and right pole come forward in **B.** A full stride with the left foot is completed in **C,** and in **D** the right foot begins to come forward through **E** and **F.** The right foot then pauses again in **G** as the left foot glides ahead again in **H.** ERWIN A. BAUER.

A   **B**

These pictures illustrate the proper position of body and thrust past with both poles at the same time. ERWIN A. BAUER.

A word of advice about handling the poles: Try to grip the handles firmly rather than too tightly. Try to assume what could be called a relaxed grip, keeping in mind that later traveling over rougher terrain may alter that somewhat.

After you have mastered the natural ski glide, the next step is learning to turn and to stop. Even left to your own devices, without any instruction, you would soon discover how to do these things. But read on anyway, for you might find a short-cut to progress.

HOW TO TURN

To turn, starting from a standing position, all you have to do is step around to another direction, one ski at a time, being careful not to step on one planted ski with the other. This is usually called the star turn, from the pattern it leaves in the snow. This simple and basic movement can early be adapted to turning while you are gliding along at slow speeds. Gliding with skis parallel, swing one ski out (the one on the side you plan to turn toward) and plant it in the new direction. Immediately swing the other (outer ski in the

turn) and plant it parallel to the first. All this can be achieved while maintaining some momentum forward. Repeat the lifting and planting of skis as often as necessary to be faced in the new direction. This is called a step-turn; with practice it will come very easily to any beginner.

A little more difficult and requiring more practice is the skating turn. It differs from the previous step in that the skier *pushes off from* one ski and lands on the other pointed in the new direction.

Assume you are gliding along, weight distributed equally on both skis, and you want to turn left. From a slightly crouching position, shift the weight onto your right ski, lift the left ski, and with the right leg push the left ski off in the new direction. With weight shifted onto the left ski, quickly bring the right ski parallel to it. This turn also becomes second nature with practice, but it should be practiced first at very slow glides with only slight changes of direction. It is a maneuver that will come much more easily to those with experience at ice skating and roller skating.

After you feel at ease on the level, it is time to tackle more rolling real estate, to learn to travel uphill and downhill as well. Skiing downhill is mostly a matter of staying relaxed and limber as confidence in gliding down slopes builds up. But first let's see about getting on top of the slopes.

A

B

C

D

This sequence shows the proper way to execute a step-turn from a standing position, facing in one direction, so as to turn 180 degrees on the spot. ERWIN A. BAUER.

If the hill is not too steep and the skis are properly waxed, it is possible to proceed directly up a slope. ERWIN A. BAUER.

But if the hill is too steep to go straight up, select a diagonal route up any slope. UTAH TRAVEL COUNCIL AND ERWIN A. BAUER.

HOW TO CLIMB

If skis have been properly waxed (see Chapter 3), it will be possible to ski-step (to walk, really) right up the face of moderate slopes. You may even be able to kick out and glide up the slope, shortening each stride to suit the degree of incline. If going straight up proves too steep and you start sliding backward, try turning slightly to one side or the other and going up diagonally—at not such a steep grade. It helps in any uphill skiing to lean the body forward exactly as if you were walking up a steep hill.

If a hill becomes too steep to proceed even on an angle (diagonally), one alternative is the herringbone step, obviously named after the pattern of ski-prints left in the snow. You walk uphill as if you had very flat feet (skis not parallel, but placed at an angle), placing skis alternately ahead of each other at about a ninety-degree angle—so that you form a series of ninety-degree V shapes up the slope. Poles are used mostly to stop backward sliding rather than to push upward.

For some skiers (mostly the less lithe and limber), herringboning very far is difficult and very tiring. For them, and for anyone on slopes too steep to herringbone, sidestepping is the best way to negotiate a hill. This is exactly like walking up a staircase sideways, with skis kept parallel. You lift the uphill ski first, plant it firmly, then bring the lower ski up and plant it parallel just below. Then move the uphill ski again, and so forth. Use the ski poles to help establish each position as you go. The steeper the hill, the shorter must be your uphill steps. You may also have to flex your knees to get a better grip on the sidehill snow.

To get up very steep places, use the side step, which is exactly like walking up a staircase sideways. ERWIN A. BAUER.

The proper stance for most downhilling: legs spread wider apart than normal in forward skiing and knees bent. ERWIN A. BAUER.

Downhill skiing viewed from the front. Note again that knees are flexed. ONTARIO MINISTRY OF INDUSTRY AND TOURISM.

GOING DOWNHILL

Going downhill requires more confidence and less musclepower than going up. It is also a lot more fun. Start out slowly at first on low hills, and increase to steeper slopes only as confidence permits. The proper position or stance for downhilling is with knees and ankles bent to act as shock absorbers. Most instructors advise downhilling with one ski slightly ahead of the other.

After managing modest hills, with knees bent, relaxed, and with weight distributed evenly on both skis, try shifting all your weight first onto one ski, then onto the other as you go down. Many ski-touring instructors advise doing this in a slow and easy rhythm, both for the additional confidence it gives and as a prelude to other steps and maneuvers. When a slope is too steep to go down straight, look for a diagonal route down and round the slope to the bottom.

HOW TO STOP

A term as familiar to skiers as the herringbone is the snowplow. The snowplow is the best, most efficient means of stopping a glide or a downhill run. It is named for the V position of the skis, with points forward and inward, which plows up snow in a breaking process. Usually, the softer the snow surface, the better it works. Following is how to do it correctly.

You are speeding downhill. Your weight, with knees and ankles bent, should be evenly on both skis. To slow down, press (force) the heels outward until your skis form a V-shaped snowplow. By all means hold your poles pointing backward, and do not try to brake by poking them into the snow ahead; this can result in a spill or injury if you are going very fast.

The braking effect of the V skis can be increased by assuming a knock-kneed position and spreading the ski tails farther apart, a position that plows up more snow. A word of warning is required here. Before depending on a snowplow to stop a headlong rush on a very steep slope, practice it frequently on slighter slopes. Learn ex-

Demonstrating the snowplow position of the skis in braking downhill. EDWIN A. BAUER.

actly how much braking is necessary to bring you to a stop, no matter what the snow condition. (The harder-packed the snow, the harder to stop.) It is one of those things that come from experience rather than written instruction.

It is possible to turn—even fairly sharply in some snow conditions—when you are snowplowing. To make such a turn, you assume the same snowplow position just described, weight evenly on both skis. To turn right, shift your weight onto the left ski, because that one will be pointed toward the right side. The more it is weighted, the sharper the turn, but this may be limited by the speed you have attained or by the degree of the slope. Shifting weight is accomplished by leaning out and over the ski—over the left ski if you are turning right. Again, the ski poles should be held pointed toward the rear.

Braking down a long, fairly steep slope is best done by snowplowing alternately left and right, going from one turn into the other. To stop completely, you can continue one turn almost 180 degrees until you are almost facing uphill, at which time progress will stop. It should be re-emphasized here—again—that poles should not be used in trying to effect a stop when you are going down a steep hill.

Up to this point I have described all the techniques necessary for a skier to travel—even to lope, under perfect conditions—over a variety of terrains easily and safely. Almost all of them are techniques that come almost naturally; a beginner might learn them himself without instruction or reading at all. In addition, there are a few other techniques that can help an advanced skier to attain greater speed and mobility. One is called double poling.

HOW TO DOUBLE-POLE

Double poling is using both arms/poles at once—in unison—rather than alternately, as in the normal ski tour glide. It can be done with or without the leg kick. It is most often a means of picking up speed on gentle downhills or on the level. When the regular kicking motion is added, this technique usually is called double-pole striding.

To double-pole (while gliding, without stride), begin by planting both poles in the snow with the shafts straight up and down (vertical) about an arm's length in front of the upright body. Next, bend at the waist and knees, and while you are moving forward, use body weight on the poles to give a forward thrust. It's important that the body and not the arms provide most of that thrust. It is only after you have passed the planted ski poles that the arms push against the poles, and you finish with arms and poles in a straight line behind, from shoulder to pole tip.

To double-pole while striding, swing both arms forward in unison, at the same time kicking forward on the right ski. The kick should end when the arms are fully forward. Plant the poles as the right ski comes parallel to the left ski. Otherwise it's the same, roughly, as when you are gliding. We say "roughly" because few experienced skiers do the double-pole stride the same way twice. Instead, they use it to accelerate whenever necessary to suit the travel over an uneven or broken terrain. After you have practiced and become familiar with the double-pole technique while gliding, it eventually becomes second nature to incorporate the double pole into a ski-touring stride whenever it will help.

ADVANCED TURNS

There are several different ways in which advanced cross-country skiers can turn. They are known as the tacking turn, stem turn, and kick turn. The kick turn, which is only recommended for the most agile, permits a standing skier to do an about-face quickly and end up pointed in the opposite direction. The tacking turn (named after a sailing maneuver) permits a skier to go zigzagging up a hill in a manner similar to switchbacking up a steep trail on foot. The stem turn, which should be attempted only after mastering the basic snowplow, permits turning on a downhill run without losing speed. None of these three techniques can be suitably described on the printed page. It is far better to have an expert instructor demonstrate them properly.

Skiing with a load in a backpack will at first seem somewhat more precarious than without carrying a weight. The steeper and more uneven the terrain, the more unsteady a beginner (especially) might feel. But by starting first with a light pack and gradually increasing the load, a skier soon forgets that he is carrying a cargo. Of course, a well-balanced pack that fits the skier's body well is far better than one that does not. Anyone who can pack a load along a summer foot trail can pack the same weight on a ski trail. Some claim it's even easier over snow.

HOW TO FALL
AND HOW TO GET UP

COMMON OBSTACLES

Any beginner (and any advanced skier) can figure on taking his share of spills during the learning process. Few spills, however, are ever very serious, and most of them merely involve digging out of a soft snowbank and somehow getting upright again. There are more different ways to fall than could be listed in one book, and I have probably experienced them all. So will anyone who spends much time on touring trails.

The deeper and softer the snow, the more cushioned will be the fall. Also, the harder it will be to get back on two skis again. The first step is to try to draw your skis directly underneath you and then slowly to stand erect. If there are others nearby, a helping hand or two make this very easy. Lacking assistance, try to use the poles for support in getting up. Lay one pole on top of the other and use it as a lever. Maybe a tree or sapling is handy for support.

If you end a spill very deeply imbedded in a snowbank, it may be necessary to remove the skis. In a soft situation such as this, you will not be able to stand on your feet alone without sinking in. First extricate the skis and place them flat on top of the snow, one on each side of you. Use your arms and the skis to raise yourself up above snow level and into a vertical position onto the skis. Often the poles (crossed) also can be used as levers when they are placed flat on the snow's surface.

Most of the time when you are traveling along at a normal pace or when you are gliding downhill, a fall can be anticipated. You *know* you are going down. In this case make it a "controlled" fall by going down as gently as possible. If you are downhilling without a reasonable chance to stop upright, aim for the nearest soft snowbank, squat down low on the skis, relax, and try to enjoy it.

Of course, spills and other problems can be avoided by being careful where you go—and how. Stay away from slopes that are too steep. Always watch for fences (especially wire fences) that may be hidden under the snow; to catch skis under a fence while downhilling can result in the ugliest kind of tumble. (A hidden barbed-wire fence may be the single greatest danger of cross-country skiing in agricultural areas.) If a fence is visible in your path, stop and either remove your skis to cross it or do it by the step-turn method.

Be careful when you are crossing wooden bridges, because either the skis or ski pole can get stuck in planking or actually break off if you are moving too rapidly. Early and late in the season, particularly, streams or pools of shallow water may have to be crossed. But before plunging your skis into the water, look for alternatives, such as removing the skis and crossing via stepping-stones or by jumping. If skis get wet at certain temperatures and are planted in snow after a water crossing, they may ice up. Removing the ice can be a next-to-impossible headache in the field.

How much skiing is enough for you? How far can you, should you, safely go in the beginning? That depends on previous physical conditioning, of course, but the following rules of thumb (a consensus of several internists and heart specialists who are serious skiers) are worth keeping in mind. Probably the ideal, most healthy amount of skiing is the amount that leaves you relaxed and happily and pleasantly tired (even drowsy or sleepy) after a session on skis (or snowshoes, for that matter). Of course, you can figure on some stiffness and soreness in the joints after a good workout, but this should disappear after a hot bath, shower, or sauna. To ski beyond that—so that you end up with really sore and nagging muscles that do not respond to heat—means that you've stretched a good thing too far. Slow down the pace until you are more fit and enjoy it more.

But minor spills and sorenesses notwithstanding, learning to cross-country ski is easy. With experience under your belt it becomes pure pleasure. Fortunately, anybody who can walk can also ski.

CHAPTER 5

CROSS-COUNTRY TRAILS— ON AND OFF

Most cross-country skiers in America never venture very far, if at all, from established trails. At least 95 per cent of all touring involves comparatively short trips of a day or less in length. In other words, most skiers plan to be back under shelter somewhere when night falls. Some never stray far out of sight and sound of other skiers, so that there is little chance of getting lost, and that is well and good. Fortunately, there are more miles of well-marked, safe ski trails all across northern ski country than anyone could explore, even if a lifetime were devoted to it.

In Chapters 13 and 14 I will list by state and province many of the most attractive resort facilities and trail networks for ski tourers. All these together, however, represent only a fraction of the trail mileage that exists on public lands—in national parks, monuments, and forests, as well as on other federal and state-owned lands. For the most part, the trails are the hiking trails of summertime, which are kept open throughout the winter either by regular maintenance or simply by constant use by skiers and snowshoers. In many parks, the same maps that show hiking trails can also be used as ski guides. An exception would be in the high alpine portions of western national parks where ski touring isn't practical. To find out about the cross-country skiing on any of our federal lands, write to the area superintendents listed in the Appendixes.

NATURE TOURS

In recent years, visiting public areas has more than doubled, and a good bit of erosion by humans has taken place. It has been necessary to fence off certain natural wonders to protect them and even to close campgrounds until vegetation has a chance to regenerate. The crowding of people into popular national parks is not necessarily desirable. Winter brings a notable exception, however. Although it is not official policy to welcome one group any more than another, ski tourers are welcome wherever skiing is possible. Skiers leave nothing behind but their tracks, and the whole philosophy of Nordic skiing is one of appreciation rather than alteration of the outdoors. Skiers are not only welcome but also are encouraged as a result.

Consider Grand Teton Park as an example. Although heavy snows fall and wind builds deep drifts, enough park roads are plowed open throughout the winter to enable skiers to reach the most popular trailheads. Even if a new snowfall has obliterated old ski tracks, the trails (here as in other parks) can be followed by markers or blazes on trees well above the snow level. The main park visitor center at Moose remains open throughout the season; there a skier can find up-to-date trail information as well as a good chance

Most cross-country skiing is done in small groups over familiar marked trails of national parks and forests, as well as in state parks. Here is a trail at Saddleback Mountain, Maine. MAINE DEPARTMENT OF COMMERCE AND INDUSTRY. PHOTO BY JOHN NORTON.

When a group is skiing out after a fresh snowfall, the task of trail-breaking should be rotated among all. VERMONT DEVELOPMENT DEPARTMENT.

to warm hands and feet while he is browsing through an interesting museum.

Several times each week, nature hikes (which begin at the Moose visitor center or Colter Bay) are led by ranger naturalists. Some are intended for skiers, other for snowshoers. If you don't have your own snowshoes, the National Park Service provides good ones, as well as instruction in how to use the webs. Usually the ski hikes are of short enough duration so as not to exclude inexperienced skiers, but they are excellent introductions to a Rocky Mountain winter for anyone. Later on, more ambitious skiers can continue farther on their own—and at a faster pace. Similar ski-nature-interpretive programs are offered free at California's Yosemite Park and many others.

The best bonus of all in national park ski touring is that you can see some of the world's greatest natural wonders, at a time when they are more exquisite than ever, at your own pace and timing. It's an opportunity few other outdoorsmen have.

MAKE YOUR OWN TRAILS

In many parts of the United States, but with emphasis on the Northeast where space is at a premium, a lot of ski-touring opportunities are still being neglected. Cities, townships, and counties in every state own real estate that is not being used. Some mining companies, many utilities, and major timber companies especially, own or lease vast tracts of "undeveloped" lands. Add to these the miles upon miles of old rights-of-way, both used and abandoned. Altogether this acreage is larger than several states. Why not make the most of it?

Often the owners are anxious to have idle lands used for some benefit to the community, especially if that use does not change it or clamp some permanent label onto it. Nothing fits the case better than recreation such as cross-country skiing or snowshoeing.

In most of these idle areas, however, it will be necessary to build trails. The lands probably will be covered with second-growth vegetation,

through which a narrow path must be opened. Even though such places will quickly grow up again with disuse, permission to open paths will be required. Often the only ticket necessary is a polite request of the landlord—perhaps the town council or local county commissioners, or maybe the public-relations officer of a corporation or power company. In recent decades, utilities and many industrial concerns haven't always enjoyed the greatest public esteem, and the result often is a bending backward to regain it.

If your area lacks skiing facilities close by, start an investigation of nearby vacant lands. If a ski club doesn't already exist, organize one. Next, select a delegation of the most reasonable, influential, and persuasive members, and send them to whatever body manages the vacant land. Ask to use it for ski touring. If you are refused, only time has been lost, and you can look elsewhere. But the odds are high that any presentation of a plan for cross-country skiing or snowshoeing will be well considered, and you may even get some unexpected encouragement. It has happened many times.

With permission granted, you can begin to plan the trail, considering first who will use it. If the skiers are mostly beginners, keep the trail system (or at least one separate part of it) simple, on fairly level ground and without any dangerously steep grades. By planning wisely, you can sandwich quite a long trail or network of trails into a rather small area. Do this by following a winding, traversing, snakelike course to take advantage of the most picturesque landscapes, by passing the scenic overlooks, by making the final destination on any trail the most attractive spot possible.

It may prove a sound idea to have two separate trails: one for neophytes, one for advanced tourers. Keep in mind also that you will probably want to use all trails in both directions. Where possible, make the outgoing runs generally uphill and the return runs downhill. Don't forget in planning that ample parking space and possibly toilets (the portable, chemical ones) will be necessary near a starting place.

A ski trail need not be more than a yard-wide path cleared through a woods or brush. Avoid crossing swamps or bodies of water. The trail can easily be routed to avoid felling any trees larger than the smallest saplings, and care should always

In many places, ski trails can be laid out through forestland like this. Ski clubs should look for such spots in their neighborhoods. ERWIN A. BAUER.

be taken (when clearing any trail anywhere) to remove or change only what is absolutely essential. Ski touring is a sport that enjoys natural beauty and doesn't disturb it. Often there is an excellent chance to use existing cowpaths, logging roads, or bike or hiking trails, rather than opening up new avenues.

By taking best advantage of the terrain, by going around obstacles rather than through or over them, a crew of three or four working on weekends and spare time before the first snow falls can create a lot of trail. All the tools a crew will need are a small power saw or a two-man bucksaw, an ax, and a couple of pairs of heavy brush clippers. Teamwork gets the job done faster, and a couple of teams working in competition can work wonders. Send the brush clippers ahead first to make the first pass. The sawyers and choppers can follow with the final trail opening. (It shouldn't be missed that the trail work will get the arms and shoulders in shape for using the ski poles later on.)

Not all the work is finished when the last branches are cut, however. Every winter snowstorm will drop dead trees across paths—maybe a good many of them. These have to be removed or detoured. But wind-drifted snows can be an even greater nuisance. There may be enough steady ski traffic on trails (especially if they are near enough to towns to be used constantly) to keep the snow compacted into the best shape. But some other means may be necessary.

A single snowmobile running over the trails can make them suitable for touring, even after a heavy snow. Better still is to tow a track sled over the trails by snowmobile. Track sleds are weighted and have cutting edges (like miniature snowplows), which both set and level the snow for the smoothest, fastest skiing. They work as well on deep ruts after a thaw and freeze as after a heavy snowfall.

If a cross-country ski group has been lucky enough to obtain an area suitable for long trails and an extensive trail network, additional safety precautions must be taken. Trails should be well marked at intersections with destination and distance arrows, to keep less sophisticated skiers from getting lost. The markers need not be elaborate or expensive, but interest can be added by giving colorful local names to the trail junctions and to places along the way. If there are a good

many interested skiers, a simple map, perhaps only mimeographed to keep the cost minimal, may be prepared.

HOMEMADE NATURAL TRAILS

A number of local ski-touring clubs in New England and the northern Midwest have made their trail systems so popular that they have attracted kindred spirits from far away. Instead of laying out ski trails alone, they've made nature-ski trails.

The way to do this is to take advantage of unusual geological features, wildlife dens and den trees, big-game yarding areas, deer crossings, giant trees, and anything else that illustrates some facet of the winter environment. These features might even be inconspicuously labeled, to be noted by skiers in passing. In at least one instance, a noted naturalist was enlisted to help lay out the most instructive trail possible over lands controlled by a power company that was not a favorite of conservationists. The arrangement helped to improve relations. Another club refurbished a small, abandoned building with a stone fireplace and made it into a warming place and a neat trailside nature museum. Youth groups were encouraged to ski the trails to the cabin, where a club member lectured briefly on the nature exhibits and the conservation ethic.

NIGHT TOURS

Few experiences are more memorable than a ski tour through a cold, clear, still, star-studded moonlit night. The outdoors at that time is a different world from any that a skier has seen before.

A night trip should be carefully planned. The party should be small and well selected; never assemble a loud or boisterous group. The route should be thoroughly reconnoitered by at least one responsible person, and if necessary it should be marked with colored streamers. This is no time for anyone to stray and become lost; after dark, temperatures on clear nights can drop thirty degrees or more below daytime averages.

If the tour is planned for an area (other than national parks) where dead wood is abundant and where campfires are permitted short of destruction to the environment, ski out by daylight to a night destination and gather a supply of firewood. Select a place to build a fire and either clear all the snow from it or tramp down the snow until it is very hard. Stack the firewood there, cover it up, and be sure you can find it again in the dark. Then, on the first, clear night with a full (or nearly full) moon, ski out to that place with your friends.

Even for those who have skied often at night, such a run over dry, crystal snow will prove unbelievably exhilarating. It has been compared to skiing across a planet light-years away on which no one else had ever set foot. If it is in the East, you might see the yellow lights from a farm window flicker on and off behind the trunks of trees in passing. In the more wide-open West it is easier to glide out beyond the range of electricity, but one sound that might be heard is the haunting song of coyotes who are also on a night run. The handsome wild dogs are only communicating with one another and are never a danger to humans.

On reaching the cache of wood, start a fire as quickly as you can and nobody will notice or care if you use some kind of artificial starter for expediency. Then sit around the blaze for a short while and cook or eat whatever somebody has brought along for the purpose. There is one sad thing about this scene: The fire will soon burn down, and it will be time to turn homeward again. But too long a pause out there will only result in chilling anyway.

Some words of restraint should be inserted here. The temptation will always be to travel too far—to range too widely—on a magic winter's night. Restrict the trips to modest length for average skiers; one to two miles each way is plenty. Keep everyone together always and discourage any exploration, because moonlight isn't nearly as bright as it seems, and getting lost can suddenly turn a lark into a horror. Sage advice that probably will go unheeded is to save the alcoholic drinking until the very end of the trip. Boozing just doesn't mix with night skiing any better than it does with driving on icy roads. The most serious ski-touring tragedy I know about involved a night party that, drinking, became lost. Three of six froze to death without knowing that they were within a quarter mile of their starting point.

Night skiers should wear somewhat warmer clothing than during daytime. At least they should carry along a thick down jacket and warmup pants to slip on during any breaks in the trip. Equipment should also be checked well before starting out. Skis should be properly waxed in the comfort of a warm place. It might even be the same place you can luxuriate in a sauna at the end of the trip.

OFF-TRAIL TRAVEL

Eventually the whole thrill of the sport for some skiers will be in getting away from the established trails, the farther the better. That is an attitude easy to understand. And anyone who is capable of handling it is not to be discouraged. Capable, in this case, means being able to cope with emergencies and especially not to get lost. Wandering even a short distance from trails in remote, mountainous, wooded, or unfamiliar country involves risks. It is risky to depart far from traveled paths even in familiar country, because sudden storms and the onset of darkness can drastically alter the looks of any place. Landmarks can vanish in gloom, and then every direction looks the same.

So let's concede here that getting lost is always a possibility. There is no need, however, for a physically fit and competent skier or snowshoer to fear traveling in strange places as long as he proceeds sensibly.

The first rule of cross-country travel is to know where you are going. Never head anywhere without a reliable compass and a map of the area, preferably a topographical contour map. Many compasses ranging from cheap to very costly are available on the market, but one that we've found ideal for cross-country skiing is the Sportsman, made by Uncle Mike's (Michaels) of Portland, Oregon. Although it fits in a pocket or can be

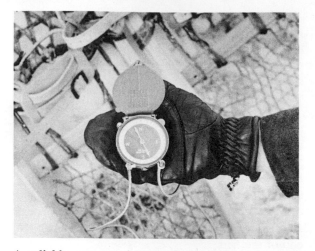

A reliable compass is essential for any skier who leaves established trails. This is the Sportsman, made by Michaels of Oregon. ERWIN A. BAUER.

carried around the neck on a rawhide thong, the Sportsman is a precision instrument that permits a tourer to compensate for magnetic declination (which varies as much as thirty-three degrees from true north in certain parts of North America). Other compasses do not have this feature. The Sportsman retails for about $20.

Obviously, carrying a compass isn't enough; the carrier should know how to use it with confidence. Most compasses include an instruction sheet containing enough information to show a skier the general direction in case of doubt. Study this sheet and carry it in a hip pocket. Besides, anyone planning a more ambitious cross-country trip had better get out and practice over-snow navigation well beforehand. Better still, obtain a copy of Bjorn Kjellstrom's *Be Expert with Map and Compass,* published by Charles Scribner's Sons at $6.95 in paperback.

The way to obtain topographical maps of any skiing area is first to request the free index map of the states, available from two distribution centers. For state indexes east of the Mississippi River (including Minnesota), write to the U. S. Geological Survey, 1200 S. Eads St., Arlington, VA 22202. For western state indexes write USGS, Federal Center, Denver, CO 80225. With the index in hand, it is easy to select exactly which topographical sheet or sheets you will need. In many areas where cross-country skiing (or hiking, backpacking, or packtripping) is popular, topographical maps of local ski-touring areas will be for sale in ski, mountain, and sporting goods shops. They sell for about $2.00 each. Trail maps of many national forests are available free at forest headquarters or ranger stations. Trail guides are also published for many regions; check the Appendixes for a list of these.

In addition to carrying the map and compass, a skier who contemplates leaving trails should notify others of his exact plans. In case he does not return, help can be sent to find him. If he is skiing in a national park, the skier should register at park headquarters; in national forests he should register at the nearest ranger station. Around busy downhill ski areas, it is wise to notify the local ski patrol of one's plans—or at least tell a close friend who will be concerned if something goes wrong.

Every skier who tours alone or away from trails should have a survival kit tucked in his belt back or day pack. The kit should include at least the following items: high-calorie food snacks (such as gorp), matches and fire starter in a waterproof container, pocket knife, section of nylon rope, first-aid kit, and an extra layer of dry clothing. Spare slip-on tip ends (available in plastic) to replace tips broken from skis can be worth their weight in pure platinum when you are far from a starting point. Suntan lotion may come in very handy. Some survival manuals advise the skier to carry along a whistle and a red-colored flare, which rescue teams can use to find him if he is lost. If the trip is to be longer than a day, the skier should carry a small shovel, a shelter (a tent or at least something, with which to construct a lean-to), and other camping equipment, which will be discussed in Chapter 6.

Care should be taken to calculate distances accurately when you are contemplating a trip. Keep in mind that in the exuberance of planning, it is easy to underestimate. What appears to be perfectly level, easy terrain may turn out to be drifted with snow or blocked by steep slopes and stream crossings. Also, it may prove necessary to detour around places where the danger of an avalanche exists. Hurrying too fast to maintain too ambitious a schedule can result in overheating, which is not good when you are alone in a wilderness. If you are one of a cross-country skiing party, distances and time should be based on the slowest, least capable member of the group, never on anything else.

This leads to another point that cannot be overemphasized. Pick your trail companions well and with forethought. The longer and more grueling an expedition promises to be, the more important it is to go with people who are capable and can stand the gaff. Take short trips with prospective friends to be sure of their ability and confidence off the trails. Be sure you like them. Failure to follow this precaution may have ruined more trips and more friendships than failure of equipment, getting lost, or anything else.

Experienced cross-country skiers agree that it is foolhardy for anyone to venture beyond the point of doubt, where confidence begins to dwindle. Do not tour beyond a limit from which you are doubtful about returning. Unless a skier is prepared mentally and physically for the experience, he should avoid getting caught out after night falls in a winter woods. Just reading about it cannot describe the terror that can come with sudden darkness, plus fatigue and intense chill.

Winter across the country of the northern United States and throughout Canada is a time of angry moods and severe enough weather to test anyone, and so a survival kit can be a psychological as well as a physical need. Complete lightweight survival kits, storm kits, and storm-shelter kits are sold in many places. They are prepared and packed by, among others, the Mountain Rescue Council of Tacoma, P. O. Box 969, Tacoma, WA 98401.

The serious outdoorsman should have a knowledge of basic first aid, and ski tourers are certainly no exceptions. Every autumn at downhill skiing centers, the various ski patrols hold refresher courses in first aid, with emphasis on winter emergencies. If it is impossible to attend one of these, a skier might search out one of the free courses held closer to home by the Red Cross, local fire and emergency departments, YMCAs, Boy Scouts, state fish and game departments, and adult-education centers. For the record, cross-country skiing emergencies are much more likely to come from frostbite and hypothermia (more on this later) than from bodily injuries such as those suffered in alpine skiing. Luckily, frostbite is something that can be prevented in almost every instance.

It is good sense to plan all trips carefully, plotting the longer ones on topographical and trail maps, which are readily available. ERWIN A. BAUER.

Hands or fingers getting very cold? Swing arms vigorously in circles behind the back—alternately. A few minutes of this should warm the entire upper body. ERWIN A. BAUER.

AVOID
COLD AND FROSTBITE

Feet and fingers invariably are the first to get cold in any situation. It's a mistake to allow these extremities to become dangerously cold in the first place. If gloves or mittens aren't doing the job, a further way to warm numb fingers is to add another sweater or shirt and then to swing the arms vigorously and rapidly in full circles. Five minutes of this should warm the fingers considerably. Often, very cold hands may be an early warning signal that the rest of the body is hovering on the edge of chilling.

It is harder to warm cold toes than fingers. First try traveling more rapidly, and if that fails, try loosening up boot laces to restore circulation. Often that will help, and so will changing to dry, clean socks if it is practical. Or with boot laces left open, try jumping up and down in place. If that fails, and wood happens to be handy, stop and build a fire. Keep the blaze small, confined enough to concentrate heat on your toes while you sit close by. At the same time, rub your feet, and especially the toes. Once the toes are warm again, start skiing as soon as possible and aim for the nearest place where the whole body can be warm and comfortable.

Staying warm—avoiding frostbite—is largely a matter of proceeding at the steady pace at which you neither chill nor overheat. Do this always and avoid unnecessary problems, on or off the trails.

CHAPTER 6

CAMPING AND BACKPACKING

Although the vast majority of ski tourers are interested only in short daytime trips for pure exhilaration, there comes eventually the urge to make a longer expedition—to stay out overnight somewhere. Camping out in the wilderness in the dead of winter may just be a test and a challenge—a personal survival contest. No matter what the motivation, overnighting can prove to be either a great adventure or an ordeal, depending on how you prepare for it. Sound planning is absolutely essential, and the most important factor in any overnight trip is proper shelter from the most intense cold.

A cross-country skier can either take along his shelter or prepare it where he camps. In other words, he can carry a tent on his back or build his shelter wherever he plans to stay. The latter means either constructing an igloo or digging a snow or ice cave. More on how to build both of these later in this chapter. It is at least ten degrees warmer sleeping inside any of these shelters than sleeping outdoors in the same bag.

In a few scattered areas, a skier may be able to depend upon natural caves or caverns, or mine shafts, keeping in mind that these may not be totally safe. Or he might take temporary refuge in an abandoned cow camp or trapper's cabin. Along the trails of many government lands are ranger or guard stations, line camps or summer hiking shelters that a skier also can utilize. But no overnight cross-country trip should be undertaken without some definite shelter in mind. The leader of the party should know exactly where it is and that it may be buried (and therefore hard to find) under a drift of snow.

The best advice to a skier planning a camping trip is to try out snow camping first. It should be done experimentally near home so that, in case it becomes too tough or unpleasant, the camper can easily retreat to a centrally heated indoors. Some experienced winter campers may scoff at that advice, but it's wise nonetheless, no matter whether one is camping in a tent or otherwise. If you plan to camp in an igloo or ice cave, first practice building one as near home as possible. Try sleeping overnight and cooking in it. If you're planning to use a tent, the backyard is a good place to pitch it for a few nights of sleeping and living under canvas. Only that way can a skier know beforehand what an actual camping trip will be like.

Obviously, winter cross-country camping will require more specialized and often expensive equipment than touring alone. But a serious backpacker or mountain climber may already own everything he would need. Besides winter clothing and touring skis (not light touring or racing skis), a cold-weather camper's check list should include shelter, a bed, food and cooking gear, plus something in which to carry it all.

WINTER TENTS

Pitched in a sheltered place, the base cleared of snow and situated beyond the sweep of savage winds, a nylon backpack tent from one of the reputable manufacturers (Eureka, Gerry, Browning, Kelty, Mountain Products, North Face, Cole-

A good mountain or alpine expedition tent is a necessity for ski campers unless they plan to build an ice cave or an igloo. Try out any tent near home before going on an ambitious trip in bitter weather. ERWIN A. BAUER.

man) will serve for winter camping. Tents should have light aluminum tube framing and built-in waterproof floors. Best of all are the mountain-expedition tents of nylon designed especially for rock-bottom temperatures and high winds. There are so many of these being marketed today that I can't describe them separately, but most of them have several features in common: a low and wind-resistant silhouette, an over-the-top fly that provides insulating space between tent and fly, and a fairly high price tag.

One recent model of tent, moderately priced but excellent, is the Eureka Company's two-man Alpine Expedition tent, which has an on-the-trail weight of about eight pounds. The somewhat heavy weight is a concession to toughness and comfort in extreme temperatures. Good mountain/winter tents will run at least $200. Some of them come packed in two (rather than one) stuff bags so that the load can be shared between two skiers. Any winter tent should be uncomplicated enough to pitch quickly with cold hands and in a strong wind.

When you are purchasing a winter tent, you should check carefully for quality workmanship all around, checking especially all seams and stitching to see that sewing has been done with

Offset "igloo" tunnel opening in Eureka alpine tent is a handy feature in high winds and blowing snow. Inside is a small "vestibule" for storing gear. ER-WIN A. BAUER.

skill. Corners and other areas of stress should be reinforced. The peak of a winter blizzard is no time to spring a leak or a rip. Look for the double-wall feature, which may be cataloged by some manufacturers as a tent with fly; this provides the air space between two walls. Air space prevents the breathing of occupants from precipitating inside the tent and causing a disagreeable moisture problem. Dampness is to be avoided. Look for shock-cord ties running from all around the tent sides to the ground; these help to absorb the shock of gusting winds. A winter tent should also include extra-long plastic or metal U-shaped stakes for anchoring the tent firmly into a frozen surface. Never depend on finding stake material where you camp, and remember that driving *any* stake may be very difficult.

SLEEPING BAGS

You cannot enjoy ski camping without getting a good night's sleep *every* night, and this is possible only with a warm sleeping bag and a pad or mattress beneath it. Of all equipment used in winter camping, a sleeping bag is the most important. Never skimp in buying one.

A suitable winter bag is one that is *lightweight* and compressible to small size (bulk) for packing on the trail. It should be water-repellent, warm, and able to "breathe"—to allow body moisture to escape rather than accumulating inside. Fitting these specifications are a large number of bags in goose- or eiderdown or Dacron, fashioned into either mummy (body- or form-fitting) shape or rectangular shape. The down-filled bags remain the warmest of all per weight of insulating material used, and therefore they are probably the more desirable. But down is also more expensive than such synthetics as Dacron Fiberfill II. With availability decreasing and the cost of down skyrocketing, the synthetics just might be a skier's best buy in bags today. There is no shortage of Fiberfill II, for instance, and it remains comparatively inexpensive. It is mildew-resistant, nonallergenic, machine-washable, tumble-dryable, durable, and odorless. So the choice between Dacron and the lighter, fluffier down is purely personal—or economic.

The unzippered mummy shape is warmer and more efficient per weight of insulation for really cold situations, but it does have drawbacks. Many people cannot sleep comfortably with their feet always close together, as they must be in a mummy. A nylon zipper that opens at either end may solve the problem of comfort for some sleepers. But generally the answer to a mummy bag's confinement is the rectangular shape; there is some heat loss, but there is more room and "maneuverability" for the sleeping body. The warmth of any bag can be increased if the sleeper wears some or all of his clothing inside it.

A really reliable cold-weather bag should contain four or more ounces of down or Dacron fill and should be constructed of overlapping V-tube compartments or slant-tube compartments. These are forms of quilting, and they distribute the down or Dacron fill evenly throughout the bag and keep it from lumping in spots. The bag should also have what is called the "differential cut," which reduces the possibility of cold spots around hips and elbows. Zippers should be large, smooth-working, and of nylon rather than metal.

Among the better manufacturers and distributors of high-quality winter bags are Gerry, Sierra Designs, Arctic Designs, High Country, Hirsch-Weis, North Face, J. C. Penney, Camp Seven, and Camp Trails. Many of these firms also produce double sleeping bags, which compatible partners can zip together, more than doubling the warmth of the occupants. Many serious skiers consider these the greatest inventions since skis. Even when skiers are sleeping in separate bags, some warmth can be retained by grouping them side by side.

MATTRESSES

More than a sleeping bag is necessary for a good night's sleep in a winter camp. All but the most rugged—or most exhausted—skiers will want some kind of simple mattress or pad for comfort as well as for additional insulation against frozen ground. Some cross-country winter travelers still carry light inflatable air mattresses, but the popularity of these is declining rapidly as

A foam pad mattress that stretches from shoulders to hips is important for a good night's sleep. The pad is good, soft insulation between the sleeping bag and the cold ground. ERWIN A. BAUER.

opposed to polyurethane foam pads. The latter cannot be punctured and deflate during the night, and they provide a better barrier against cold from the ground. All that is necessary is a yard-wide pad of foam long enough to stretch from hips to shoulders, which are the main pressure points (and cold-transmission points) during sleep. A one-inch-thick pad is usually sufficient; some skiers may prefer two-inch or three-inch thicknesses for the added luxury.

BACKPACKS

Ski tourers who also are summertime backpackers can use the same carriers for camping gear in winter. A bewildering number of backpacks in all price ranges are now available in sporting goods stores, and the best have two things in common: aluminum tube framing and extremely light weight. These differ mostly in the shape or contouring of the frame—in how they fit onto the back, in whether the load is concentrated onto a packer's shoulders or his hips, or somehow is distributed between the two. No one style or design seems to suit all backpackers best (for they also come in many different sizes, shapes, and physiques); as with skis, it is a good idea for the ski tourer acquiring his first pack to try out several (fully loaded) before making a final selection.

An increasingly popular backpack for many skiers is a long and narrow carrier that "rides" snugly lower on the back than a summer packsack and that is called a body pack. Without exterior aluminum framing to interfere with arm freedom, this carrier is mostly for greater balance over irregular terrain because the center of gravity of man and load is lower. Nowadays many experienced ski packers are selecting teardrop-shaped body packs with sewn-in compartments to prevent shifting of weights while traveling.

A winter pack should be of waterproof (not just water-resistant) nylon. Furthermore, it should be well tested before use for balance and comfort when you are starting out on an ambitious trip. Check the seams especially, because it may be necessary to apply a permanent waterproof sealing material, even on some expensive packs. Especially with numb fingers, zippers are easier to open and close than straps and buckles, and so you should look for this type of fastening. Zippers should be large, however, and of nylon rather than metal, each one covered over with a protective flap. In some instances the new Velcro sealers are adequate for backpack flaps.

The author carrying winter camp on the same Coleman backpack used on summertime trails. However, some winter packers find the exposed frame interfers with free arm movement. PEGGY BAUER.

A narrow body pack without exposed frame allows freedom of movement and is preferred by many skiers. ERWIN A. BAUER.

Breaking trail with a winter backpack can be hard work in the mountains. PEGGY BAUER.

A mountain camper uses a Sigg cooker to melt snow before preparing a dinner of freeze-dried foods. ERWIN A. BAUER.

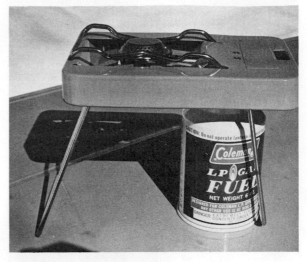

A simple collapsible burner that fits onto an LP gas cartridge and into any backpack. ERWIN A. BAUER.

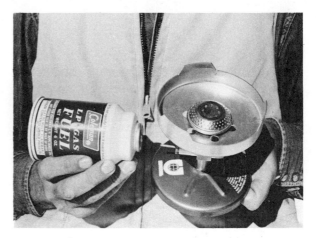

Universal cooker that uses LP cartridge also unscrews and fits neatly into backpack compartment. ERWIN A. BAUER.

COOKING GEAR

A small stove is much more practical for snow-camp cooking, despite its weight, than is dependence on firewood. Little if any wood may be available above the snow, and in some parks and wilderness areas collecting firewood is not permitted anyway. In addition, you can't build an open fire in a tent, which is the most likely refuge after a long day on a cold trail. Stoves are available that burn kerosene, gasoline, alcohol, butane, propane, and "canned heat" (Sterno). A majority of mountain skiers, however, prefer a gasoline stove with a pump. Kerosene is suitable, but it has a bad odor in the confines of a tent. Alcohol does not give sufficient heat. Butane freezes when the temperature falls below fifteen degrees Fahrenheit.

Two of the most popular stoves with ski tour guides today are the Optimus 111B, an old favorite that weighs 3½ pounds, and the newer Phoebus 625, which weighs 2½ pounds. Both use white gasoline or Coleman fuel. Either stove can solve the cooking needs for two campers at a time. A third choice might be the Primus Grasshopper, which heats with propane. Many smaller Optimus stoves for kerosene and white gas are available. So are small aluminum flasks and bottles in which to carry spare fuel. More and more stoves that use LP gas cartridges are appearing on the market.

Some words of advice about the care and safe handling of stoves should be inserted here. Always start and generate stoves outside tents and enclosed places. Keep the flame below maximum output for fuel economy and to prevent overheating (steaming) the interior of a small tent. Provide ample ventilation when you are cooking in a confined place, especially inside a nylon mountain tent. Stoves should be refueled only when they are cool; fuel or LP gas cartridges should never be replaced until they are empty. Check regularly to be certain that the burner plate of a stove is not loose or missing; the unit will be inoperable without it.

Normally, one or two aluminum pans plus aluminum utensils will be sufficient for hastily cooking a trail meal. Some skiers like to include a teakettle. Also available and becoming popular are such trail cookers as the aluminum Sigg, a nesting pan set that couples with a Svea alcohol stove. It weighs a little more than two pounds. Another convenient item is the Swedish-made Trangia storm cooker, which even works outdoors in a wind and weighs less than three pounds.

A Sigg cooker and a matching Svea stove (here disassembled into nesting parts), a current favorite of ski campers. ERWIN A. BAUER.

Optimus mountain stove, which uses white gasoline, has served well on countless mountain and cross-country ski trips for many years. ERWIN A. BAUER.

Used wisely, an aluminum container of fuel will cook many meals during a cross-country camping trip. ERWIN A. BAUER.

Freeze-dried foods prepared by several manufacturers come in an almost endless variety. One problem is that they are expensive. ERWIN A. BAUER.

A few packets of freeze-dried foods, which altogether weigh less than two pounds, can serve for one overnight trip for two on the trail. ERWIN A. BAUER.

TRAIL FOODS

Perhaps nothing during the recent history of backpacking and camping, winter or summer, has made the sport more pleasant than the introduction of freeze-dried foods. Such brand names as Mountain House, Rich Moor, Chuck Wagon, Seidel's Trail Packages, Stow-A-Way, and Trail Chef have become well known for tasty, reliable products that weigh very little. These come in a seemingly unlimited variety of foods and whole menus, from lasagna and beef stroganoff to Texas chili and Mexicali corn. There is delicious "fresh" fruit and even freeze-dried ice cream in several flavors, which can be munched "dry" along the ski trail.

These packets are available in all ski and mountain shops, most sporting goods stores, expedition outfitters, and even many supermarkets. The freeze-dried packets do tend to be expensive, but they take much of the drudgery and lugging of extra weight out of overnighting in winter. For most meals a skier needs only to add water, a small amount of heat, and a short cooking time. When you are planning a trip, figure on two pounds of freeze-dried foods per day per person, or slightly more for the most hearty appetites.

It is possible to cut the cost of freeze-dried foods somewhat by buying them in quantity directly from the manufacturer. Another alternative is to buy dehydrated foods or other substitutes in supermarkets, repacking them all to single-meal size in aluminum foil or inside the aluminum cook gear.

Packing any packsack should be done carefully and with forethought, to keep the load evenly balanced. Do it well before starting out, so that you can make necessary adjustments. Beware that food packets do not break and spill over everything else.

The main point about ski overnighting, which simply cannot be overemphasized, is to make a trial run or runs first. Know your own tolerance to cold and discomfort and your equipment very well. Pilot trips should be short, under favorable weather conditions if possible, until you build up confidence. This is doubly true if you are proceeding alone or without an experienced and capable guide. In many winter sports areas it's possible to join up with groups of campers—or even to take practical courses in winter camping on skis. Take advantage of these.

A tent camp pitched high in Tetons, as headquarters for exploring remote alpine ridges. ERWIN A. BAUER.

A camp set up by the author to test winter gear. PEGGY BAUER.

TENT CAMPING

If the overnight camp is to be a tent, the site should be selected carefully; take advantage of shelter, especially shelter from high winds. Campsites in timbered places are vastly preferable to open areas, but do not pitch a tent within range of any large dead trees that might topple in a gale. Avoid at all costs locating a tent at the base of a bare snow slope or any other potential path of an avalanche or snow slide.

In very deep snow, if it is possible, clear an area as large as the floor of the tent down to bare ground. This excavation alone will provide a shelter and windbreak, as well as a more firm anchor for the tent pegs. If that is impractical, at least tramp down firmly an area of soft snow until it is compacted hard enough to hold tent pegs. Try to pick a spot not subject to great wind drifting, a condition that might cover the tent completely during a bad storm. It is all right if snow drifts (and fills in) around the sides of a tent; this may actually provide insulation and make the occupants more snug inside. But it will be harder to retrieve the pegs and strike the tent when moving. Also, the weight of snow on top of a tent is not desirable, and too much can flatten it down on the occupants.

One kind of cozy overnight shelter that is not too hard to build is the igloo of snow. Here igloo walls are going up. PEGGY BAUER.

IGLOOS

Before civilization brought prefab huts and other "conveniences" to Eskimos scattered over the Arctic, these people survived the world's most hostile environment by living in igloos—or ice houses. Backpacking ski tourers who genuinely relish the challenge of winter in the wilderness (or even close to civilization) can do the same thing. To do so, they will have to carry along a small saw, a collapsible shovel, a large-bladed knife, or, best of all, a half-disk-shaped ice knife of Eskimo design.

Constructing an igloo isn't as complicated as it may seem, but it can be hard, sweaty work. It consists of cutting or sawing out blocks of compacted snow. These should be cubes fairly uniform in size—say, one foot square or slightly larger. Large, rolled "snowballs" might be substituted. The first step is to arrange one row of cubes in a circle seven or eight feet in diameter, with a space inside large enough for two (or however many) people to sleep flat within the circle. On top of the base row, lay (as a bricklayer or stonemason would) a second row of ice cubes, with a slightly smaller diameter than the first. Continue building upward, laying row upon row of cubes, each row having a smaller and smaller diameter, until you have formed a half sphere, cone, or beehive-shaped dome.

When you have finished, cut out a low entrance on one side, away from the prevailing wind. Build a snow barrier around the entrance. Next, chink up cracks or thin places in the beehive with loose snow. Let snow drift or blow around the outside naturally, as it will. Inside, the body heat of the occupants, plus a minimum cooking fire, will keep all comfortably warm. If the camping party is large, several igloos can be constructed, joined to one another with connecting entrances. These primitive structures can be made amazingly livable and long-lasting.

A half-igloo-half-tent compromise shelter is made possible by carrying along a tent fly or sheet of waterproof cloth about six feet by ten feet in size. First build up igloo walls as described to a height of about four feet. Excavate or tramp down the area inside for more headroom. Next, cover the open top with the fly, using skis and ski poles if necessary as pins to hold this "ceiling" in place.

A handy tool for ski campers (to build an igloo or dig a snow cave) is a light, folding, infantry type shovel. This one is a military-surplus shovel. ERWIN A. BAUER.

Digging an ice cave for overnight
shelter and then waxing skis in the
warmth of sunlight at the entrance.
Care should be taken not to dig
the cave in the potential path of an
avalanche. ERWIN A. BAUER.

SNOW OR ICE CAVES

In regions of very heavy snowfalls, skiers may
find it easier and faster to build a snow or ice
cave. The first requirement is to find a compacted
accumulation of snow vast enough to enable you
to excavate a burrow or living space down and
underneath it—without fear of collapse. Even the
remotest potential avalanche site (see Chapter
12) should be avoided at all costs, because a sudden slide could too easily cover the entrance to a
cave. Search instead for fairly level sites where

the snow condition is stable and where the snow has had time to become very dense and well compacted. In such a situation, a snow cave can be every bit as comfortable and warm as an igloo or tent.

Snow caves can be dug to accommodate a group of modest size, but assuming the number is two, proceed as follows. Begin by digging an entranceway sloping down and back into the snowbank. For easiest access it should be a tunnel 3½ to 4 feet high. It's necessary to tote a shovel for this excavation; most skiers use the folding infantry type of foxhole shovel sold in military-surplus stores. The entranceway should be dug 3 or 4 feet into the snowbank.

Beyond the entrance, but at a slightly higher elevation, excavate a chamber or cubicle big enough to enable you to unroll sleeping bags completely and sit upright on the bags while cooking without being unduly cramped or crowded. The insulation provided by such a "room" is extremely good, and occupants can be very cozy, even though encased in icy walls. The reason for the downward-sloping entrance with living chamber a step or so above is to keep the wind from blowing directly into the living space and to help trap warmth inside. If a skier remains chilled or cold after a day of traveling on a subzero trail, he can soon be warmed up to a comfortable temperature by digging his own ice cave.

A camping trip on touring skis can be the most memorable time of any winter. It takes an adventuresome soul to times and places that not many others will ever know. Or it can prove to be only a terrible chore. Planning and proper preparation make the difference.

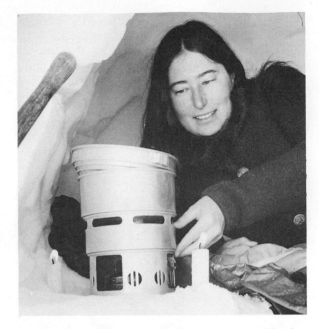

Inside an ice cave. Cooking dinner on a combination stove and using candles for illumination keep the cave cozy inside despite subzero temperatures outside. ERWIN A. BAUER.

Fluffing and drying out a sleeping bag in wind after a night's sleep. All cloth, including clothing, should be kept dry in winter camping. ERWIN A. BAUER.

CHAPTER 7

HUNTING AND FISHING

HUNTING

Let's assume it is near the end of the hunting season—and a happy ending as well. You have just bagged an elk or a moose or a large deer—a winter's supply of delicious venison for the freezer. It's a great moment and a great place. But there is only one problem, and it is major.

Snow already covers the ground, and more is falling. The field-dressed animal weighs several hundred pounds, and camp is a half day's hike or more away. Before you can relax, you have to get the meat to camp or to a cold-storage processor somewhere. When it is quartered and loaded onto a packboard, lugging the quarters through soft and deepening snow on foot will be an ordeal. If too much more snow falls, you may not be able to do it at all.

There are several solutions, and if you are in the West, a pack horse is one of the most obvious. So is the snowmobile. But neither kind of horsepower is always available, and in many hunting areas the use of snowmobiles is either illegal or made impossible by the roughness of terrain. So that leaves skis and snowshoes with which you can travel quickly on top of the snow instead of slogging through it.

Of all outdoor sportsmen, few can make better use of cross-country equipment than hunters and fishermen. The thin skis provide a means of getting into the best, most remote country at a period when it is best to do so. Also, they can greatly ease the big-game hunter's chore of getting his venison from forest to food locker.

Skis or snowshoes offer the best way for late-season rabbit hunters to get around in the northern United States and southern Canada. ERWIN A. BAUER.

All across the northern United States and throughout Canada, the best big-game hunting of all doesn't begin until many open seasons are about to close—when many species of animals have had the time to migrate downward toward winter ranges from their summer pastures in the highest places. Normally the same deep snow that drives them lower and lower (where food is more available) also makes hunting on foot more

Skis or snowshoes are handy for taking a hunting camp off the beaten track—and also for carrying meat and trophies out of the woods. ERWIN A. BAUER.

difficult. Even the best-conditioned man cannot cover too much distance afoot while he is sinking into a foot of snow with each step. He soon wears out.

On light touring skis it's another matter. Now a nimrod can greatly extend his hunting range, gliding quietly, and at the same time he can have the advantage of sighting his dark quarry against a background of white. Game is far more visible after a snowfall than viewed against the neutral greens and browns of a late autumn forest. Under average deep-snow conditions, a person can cover three or four times more distance on skis than on foot while expending the same physical energy.

In many areas, the season for hunting snowshoe hares or jackrabbits extends well into the winter. Invariably it's done with beagles or other hounds that can chase the target across a snowpacked landscape. But in many cases, unless he is on skis or snowshoes, a hunter, being heavier than hounds or hares, cannot follow them; he'll sink hopelessly.

Perhaps the most exciting and uncertain of all winter hunting is for foxes in fairly open country of the northern plains or even across agricultural lands. The object here is to begin early in the morning in search of very fresh fox tracks made late during the night—and then to follow them with a rifle and a lunch of high-calorie, high-energy foods.

To score, the skier must follow the fox tracks relentlessly, no matter where they lead or how far, meanwhile always watching far ahead toward the horizon for even the most brief glimpse of red fur streaking across white fields. Because the North American red fox is a cautious and wary animal, success at this game is very, very low; a skier must be very persistent to get a fleeting shot. But it is a great challenge and a fascinating way to spend a day on the snow. Besides tracking the fox, the skier will see many other things—winter deer yards, crow roosts, bird's nests stripped of summer's green camouflage, the place where a grouse roosted overnight in a snowbank—that a stay-at-home can never enjoy.

Over vast areas of the North, for centuries, trapping—running traplines—has been made possible only by snowshoes. The typical trapper must cover great distances, often following meandering streams, to check and reset all his traps while carrying a good bit of gear on his back. During the past few years, skis have often replaced snowshoes to reduce the travel time.

Hunter on skis tours quietly through winter wonderland where game is often easy to spot. ERWIN A. BAUER.

FISHING

But strange as it must seem, skis may be far more valuable to fishermen than to hunters or trappers, simply because their use can open up whole new worlds of fishing.

In the first place, fishing is better in winter than in summer; official creel censuses (surveys to determine the number of fish taken per hour spent angling) taken by the fish and game departments of states from Maine to Montana have revealed a much higher angling success after summertime anglers have gone home. With many popular species of fish (bluegills, crappies, walleyed pike, yellow perch, and others), the success ratio often improves after a crust of ice covers lakes. That is also the period when fishing pressure is very light —it isn't necessary to share a fishing hole with many fellow fishermen. The main point is that an outdoorsman on skis can have a good bit of excellent sport exclusively to himself all winter long. It may just be a matter of spending winter weekends, ice tackle in a pack or rucksack (maybe carrying an ice auger instead of a ski pole in one hand?), and exploring. Then stake a claim wherever you find the fish biting.

A lot of the larger and better-known bodies of water are easily accessible to snowmobilers. On these, whole ice-fishing villages will form. But the best advice is to avoid the congestion as seriously as you avoid the busy downhill ski slopes and instead seek out smaller waters that others avoid. There are the ice-locked farm ponds, for example, of which more than a million (which are fishable) are scattered over the snow belt of the United States. In some regions there are beaver ponds—the same ones around which clouds of mosquitoes and dense brush discourage summertime fishermen, but where plump brook trout are eager to strike any small jig or grub. Just stop and think for a moment about any inaccessible spots you may have had trouble fishing during the past peak seasons. Why not try them again in winter?

Frozen waters are not the only ones that beckon to skiers, however. Throughout the West, especially, flow the larger, blue-ribbon trout rivers where the legal seasons remain open—although angler access is so difficult that they might as well be closed. Snow either piles up or

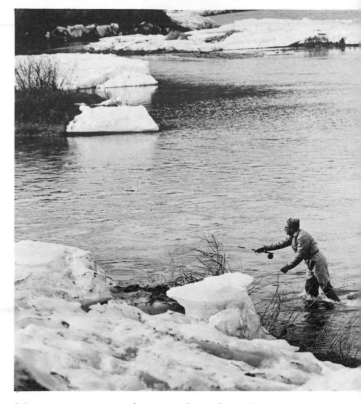

Many great western rivers (such as the Yellowstone here) are inaccessible to trout fishermen except by ski or snowshoe. ERWIN A. BAUER.

On skis it's possible to explore for remote ponds, beaver dams, and similar fishing holes that others overlook in winter. ERWIN A. BAUER.

A fine fat rainbow trout is the reward of a skier who can reach nearly inaccessible pools locked up by winter. ERWIN A. BAUER.

drifts to such depths along the banks that reaching water's edge is out of the question unless you go on cross-country skis (or snowshoes). On skis and snowshoes you can have miles and miles of the finest trout water all to yourself—if you don't mind casting into a cold wind. Of course, the line may also freeze onto your rod guides and reels may not work too smoothly, but these are only small handicaps.

Not too much has been written about midwinter trout fishing, but a few helpful points can be made. If you are skiing fairly long distances to reach the water, carry your tackle in a rucksack and your rod still encased, especially if the trail winds through forest or brush. Keep in mind that the same multipiece pack rods used for summertime backpacking to mountain lakes are suitable here. Use sinking rather than surface flies, especially weighted (the bodies) nymphs and streamers, perhaps even at the end of a sinking flyline. Many western winter trout fishermen also use what (in Montana) are called snowflies;

these are really the tiny (size 18, 20) imitations of midges that hatch on the Yellowstone River and elsewhere on certain sunny days toward the tag end of winter.

No matter whether trout are legal or not on many western rivers, there is fast fishing for whitefish, a productive sport too often overlooked. Whitefish are natives and usually bottom feeders; they are superabundant in some rivers, often (some biologists believe) to the detriment of trout. But the species has two important advantages: Whitefish strike readily on a wide variety of flies, and never more willingly than when the landscape is covered with white; also, they are among the finest food fishes, doubly so when they are slowly smoked over a "cold" hardwood fire. Among the snacks most relished on cross-country ski trips are the smoked filets of whitefish obtained on previous ski fishing trips.

Look for the most productive whitefish holes (they are usually the deepest places around sharp bends) by skiing parallel to the river. On some

A large northern pike is the prize of a skier who found a forgotten lake where the species was striking. ERWIN A. BAUER.

days, if the angle of sunlight is correct, it may be possible to see the telltale silvery flash of their bodies down in the dark blue depths. Once you find such a bonanza, keep fishing it as long as the fish strike, and have no conscience about taking too many. The legal limits are usually generous (for example, twenty-five per day in Wyoming), and the whitefish might as well be harvested.

Although it may be obvious, one important item of fishing equipment should be mentioned here: waders or hipboots. Hipboots (insulated if possible) are much preferred because they are lighter and less bulky to carry, lashed onto a rucksack or packboard. Water levels average lower in winter than in summer, and an angler in hipboots can cover a comparable amount of fishing water with his flies. But take no chances, and by all means avoid a sudden dunking—or even shipping just a little water over the tops of the boots. At the least it can be uncomfortable; at worst it can be dangerous. It is critically important in ski touring to stay dry.

Tiny midge imitations like these "snowflies" will attract both trout and whitefish during warmer days in late winter. ERWIN A. BAUER.

If you are wandering on skis far across wilderness country in search of new fishing holes, you should take all the precautions advised elsewhere in this book for off-trail travel. Leave behind a message about your plans, and always carry an emergency or survival kit. Forever thereafter you may be disenchanted with summertime fishing.

CHAPTER 8

CROSS-COUNTRY PHOTOGRAPHY

Probably no other pastime or hobby is so compatible with cross-country skiing as photography. That fact is made obvious by the vast number of skiers who carry cameras and use them. The sport simply is made to order for filming. And so are the beautiful places a Nordic skier goes.

Winter photography is not greatly different from summertime as far as composition and shooting techniques are concerned. But extreme cold and snow do present a few problems that are well to know about.

Cold itself does not harm equipment, but one thing to avoid absolutely is bringing cameras and lenses suddenly from a cold outdoors into a warm room. The resulting condensation, which appears as a fogging of the glass, can result in serious, sometimes permanent damage inside lenses and diaphragms. At the same time, leaving a camera lying lens up and facing into a bright sun is asking for trouble. Direct sunlight so focused through a lens can sear or warp the delicate parts inside and heat-damage the film.

Keep cameras and equipment dry and covered, and avoid at all costs the quick transition from a very cold to a very warm place. These two pitfalls probably account for most of the blank exposures that come back from the photofinisher.

Winter scenes in typical ski touring areas are among the most beautiful, most striking subjects a cameraman can shoot, with or without skiers in the frame. Here is a chance also for great action pictures. An experienced photographer can shoot all these instinctively—without giving much thought to what he's doing—but with not-such-experts in mind, let's go back and consider a few basics, beginning with the equipment.

As we shall see in Chapter 9, the 35mm single-lens reflex is any skier's best, most versatile bet, especially if a skier plans to aim at wildlife targets as well as his own companions and the places they ski. But for shooting winter scenes and activities alone, almost any other camera will serve at least as well. The only trouble is that the 2¼″-by-2¼″ (120-size film) cameras alone (without extra lenses) will be heavier and bulkier than the 35mms with normal (50mm) lenses alone. So take your choice and use what you already own—until you form a definite opinion that something else is better.

Especially in the beginning, take a little time when composing a winter scene. Keep in mind that what looks perfectly stunning to the eye alone might not be so on film. For example, the trail ahead winds into a foothill forest, behind which looms a magnificent range of mountains. It's the kind of inspirational setting—the calendar scene—that makes you go skiing in the first place. So you shoot it. Later your processed slide shows the trail vanishing into no place at all and the mountains only a thin line in the distance. You made the common mistake of not getting close enough to the scene.

That mistake can be corrected in two ways. The easiest is simply to ski closer until the mountains almost loom above you. Be sure they really do cover up a large part of your viewfinder. An

A party of ski tourers pauses to photograph Old Faithful geyser in winter. It is only one of countless camera opportunities in Yellowstone National Park during the "off-season." WYOMING TRAVEL COMMISSION PHOTO.

Complete loneliness and quiet of
winter can be illustrated in scenes
of winter that nonskiers seldom
see. ERWIN A. BAUER.

To shoot action, pick a suitable spot and have skiing buddies travel past you. Use a fast shutter speed. NEW HAMPSHIRE OFFICE OF VACATION TRAVEL. PHOTO BY DICK SMITH.

If a trip includes some climbing over ice, get pictures of that, too. WYOMING TRAVEL COMMISSION PHOTO.

and not just specks in the distance. If there are several have them stay close together, rather than strung out in a very long line. Concentrate on getting brightly dressed individuals in the foreground —if some are going to be closer to you than others. For most purposes, have the skiers either coming almost directly toward you (*not* going away) or going from one side to the other.

The best pictures by far are shot early and late in the day, when the sun is low. During the middle part of bright, sunny days, the light is likely to be flat, and often deceptively so. Early and late, the shadows are longer and the colors are richer. It is a magic time for a photographer to experiment with side- and back-lighted pictures, which are especially dramatic. There will be failures; even the most skilled pros have their share. But the good shots will make you forget the bad ones.

Allowing the right exposure can be a problem, but none that cannot be overcome. Dazzling bright light reflected by snow is the main culprit, complicated by incorrect use of a meter. When meters built into the camera are aimed directly onto a snowy scene, they do not always give an

alternative to skiing closer (which may not be possible) is to use a short telephoto lens. It isn't a bad idea always to use (at least) a 90mm or 135mm lens for landscapes when you are shooting scenes.

Far too often a beginning photographer does not get close enough to his people. Assume here that your plan is to shoot friends gliding along a trail or negotiating a slope. Resist trying to snap the picture on a catch-as-catch-can basis. Instead, pause and ask your friends to hold up—perhaps to go back and repeat it—so that you can get a really good picture. Now, be certain that your friends are close enough to be easily identified

Why not keep a camera handy at all times when skiing across country? Especially on bright days. Wide strap prevents camera's weight from "biting" into the neck. ERWIN A. BAUER.

accurate measurement of light on the subjects. If you are shooting a buddy, say, take the reading by holding the meter up close to his face or clothing. Then use that exposure.

Lacking a meter, the printed instruction/specification sheet that comes with every roll of film is a good exposure guide. On a dazzling bright day, use the exposure recommended for beach or snow scenes in full sunlight. To be doubly sure of important pictures you desperately want, shoot at the recommended setting and then shoot a second and third exposure after closing the lens another half and full f/stop. That is called bracketing.

Bracketing is a good idea in case of any uncertainty. Commonly used by pros who cannot afford mistakes, it is well for amateurs to copy it. When you are uncertain about an exposure, bracket by shooting the picture at several different exposures on each side of what probably is correct. Quite often some improperly exposed pictures, especially underexposures, turn out to be more appealing than those that are technically correct.

Whenever possible, try to catch the magnificent backgrounds of cross-country skiing on film. Skier adds great depth to Wyoming winter scene. ERWIN A. BAUER.

Small things along the trail—such as snow-covered pine cones—make interesting photo subjects during rest stops. ERWIN A. BAUER.

Because very bright light is a fact of much winter photography, you have the welcome option of using faster shutter speeds than normally. You should surely take advantage of it, particularly if you are shooting action. To get a fellow ski tourer sliding down a slope, you should set the camera at the fastest shutter speed possible (for the overall exposure) to stop the action. An exception would be to use an unusually slow shutter speed (say, 1/30 or 1/60 second) for deliberate blurring of the skier. But when it is possible to use a shutter speed of, say, 1/500 or 1/1000, you can compensate for your own error of camera movement.

Patterns of snow and ice crystals offer a touring cameraman chances for abstract photos. WYOMING TRAVEL COMMISSION PHOTO.

Except to achieve offbeat results, don't try to shoot while you are moving along on skis. If a picture is worth shooting, stop and do it correctly. Take advantage of the immense beauty of new snowfalls by getting out as soon as possible after weather clears. If you delay too long, wind might soon blow all the snow that has accumulated on trees, and what was a great winter scene becomes a run-of-the-mill scene.

When you are going out with friends after a new snowfall, you might ask them to let you lead the way and be the trail breaker. It won't be the most thrilling sport if the fresh fall is very deep, but it gives you the first look over completely untracked snow. When you come upon a scene that looks especially photogenic, stop and instruct your friends on how you would like them to proceed across it. Point out the exact route to take. This is how the scenes that make calendars, covers, and skiing posters are made—never by chance.

To obtain a really complete record of a skiing trip, go well beyond the usual skiing, scenic, and buddy shots. If you have a cookout, shoot at a low angle over the fire. How about a close-up of somebody munching a hotdog or drinking from a

skin bag? Camps and ice caves make fine pictures, and so do pretty faces in caps frosted with snow. Shoot when a companion waxes his skis or helps another to his feet after a tumble. Any skiing activity at all is grist for the camera.

A typical ski trip is an excellent chance for other close-ups. Check out the icicles on trees that overcanopy the trail—or for the delicate freezing patterns around waterfalls and riffles. Close-ups of frost on thistles, pine cones, and withered berries are fascinating to shoot; they also make excellent fillers in a slide presentation of a ski touring trip. Don't forget wildlife tracks. A close-up lens, bellows, or lens attachment takes up little space and adds no weight to the gear in your rucksack.

A perfectly natural question here would be, "What kind of film should I use?" The answer is that it doesn't make that much difference as long as the exposure is on the button. The bright light of sun or snow, however, makes it practical to use the slower color films; these happen to be less grainy and therefore slightly more pleasing to a critical eye.

Color—or contrast in color—should be considered when composing a picture. Skiers in darker dress are sure to stand out better when they are filmed against a snow background. But try to catch skiers wearing light, bright colors as they pass against a dark background of evergreen trees or a weathered cabin. The branches of those same evergreens, incidentally, can provide suitable screens or frames for pictures. A natural frame, usually a dark one (trees in shadow), can add great depth, beauty, and appeal to an otherwise so-so scene.

Carrying a camera can be a dividend of cross-country skiing or the main reason for doing it. The pictures can be slides projected on a screen or prints in an album. It may be hoped that, in reviewing them later, you will have remembered to focus properly, not to have cut off anybody's skis or head. Mistakes are bound to happen sometimes, and doubly so when hands are cold and the gang is clamoring for you to hurry up. There's a lot of trail winding ahead.

CHAPTER 9

SKI HUNTING WITH A CAMERA

Among the many indications that Americans have gained a greater affection for their natural environment in recent years is the expanded interest in bird and animal watching and in nature and wildlife photography. Hunting with a camera, once the exclusive business of a handful of professional photographers, is now something anyone can do well. A camera shooter is not concerned with bag limits, open and closed seasons, or any other restrictions. He can shoot rare or endangered wildlife as well as the most common species with a clear conscience. The hunting can be done near home or deep in the loneliest, faraway wildernesses.

But hunting success is seldom any better than when winter grips the land. There are several explanations for this. One is that snow and cold weather concentrate wildlife in many ways; consider the Rocky Mountains for one good example. Here such big-game animals (and great photo targets) as elk, mule deer, moose, and bighorn sheep spend summers in the loftiest altitudes where the living is easy on new green vegetation. But with the advent of fall, then winter, snow piles up in their summer range. To survive, the herds must migrate downward to where survival forage is available. That brings them within reach of a person on skis or snowshoes.

Another explanation is that almost all wildlife becomes more confiding—trusting—during bitter winters. Possibly some instinct advises animals that gun-hunting seasons have ended and the pressure is off. We do know that many large animals learn to recognize the rough boundaries of winter sanctuaries. In the Jackson Hole area where I live, elk coming from the surrounding high country are shy, wild, and at best very fleeting camera targets. But once they reach the safety of the National Elk Refuge just north of the town of Jackson, their character abruptly changes. On horse-drawn sleds it is possible to ride among thousands of wintering elk, which then show little fear of the curious humans. Admittedly this has little to do with cross-country skiing, except to illustrate an important point about wildlife behavior in favor of a skier.

The cold weather also reduces the body processes of animals—saps their strength—and they make less effort to escape an approaching person. They seem to be more tame, although that isn't the proper word for it. It is an advantage for a cameraman, but one that he should not abuse. In other words, it is a moral obligation of any photographer, on skis or otherwise, not to torment animals unduly in the struggle to survive the worst season of their lives. In many areas, winter takes a far greater toll than gunfire or other causes.

But back to skiing. Except possibly for a person on snowshoes, a skier has the advantage over any other photographer when snows are deep. A skier can cover more ground faster in his search. Besides that, skis are quiet. From our experience, a skier is more likely to arouse curiosity and alertness than suspicion or fear; it is the reverse when a snowmobiler approaches.

To watch or hunt wildlife with a camera successfully on skis, go where the wildlife is most likely to be. Carry all the photographic gear you are likely to need. That may mean much extra

A pair of bull moose encountered during a snow squall permit the author to come close enough for this photo in northwestern Wyoming. ERWIN A. BAUER.

In the Rocky Mountain West, the elk is a common target of photographers. But to find bulls fighting is especially lucky. ERWIN A. BAUER.

Elk fighting.
ERWIN A. BAUER.

weight in your pockets or on your back, but in the long run the small inconvenience will prove worth it.

Any check list of best places to hunt would include the national parks, monuments, wildlife refuges, and other sanctuaries where skiing is permitted in winter. A nationwide list of these sites would fill a volume, but a useful reference (which covers all aspects of wildlife photography anywhere, anytime) is my book *Hunting with a Camera,* published by Winchester Press, New York.

During midwinter in almost any sanctuary where the snow blanket justifies skiing, the animals will be concentrated in just a few areas—perhaps only one. Large species such as moose and deer are not likely to be far from the protective cover of evergreen trees. Search for bighorn sheep, for example, in places where strong winter winds keep feeding areas bare of snow. In areas where most lakes and waterways normally freeze, look for those scattered places where a current or warm springs maintain open water. In places like these, waterfowl, sometimes in spectacular numbers, will be jammed wing to wing, not anxious to fly.

A good example of the concentration of winter wildlife can be observed in Yellowstone National Park, which also happens to be an extraordinary spot for a camera hunting trip. The park itself, which is larger than Delaware and Rhode Island combined, covers thirty-five hundred square miles, and the big-game herds number well into five figures. But virtually all the visible wildlife that has not migrated outside the park boundaries by late fall will be concentrated in the few areas around hot springs and geyser basins and in a thin strip along the Yellowstone, Madison, and Firehole rivers, which never freeze. Come along on a typical January–February trip to see what takes place there.

Most of the high plateau is locked up under a crust of snow that may measure up to six feet thick (more during severe winters). No travel in the park is possible except from Gardiner, West Yellowstone, or Jackson (the Flagg Ranch) via daily ten-passenger snow coaches to Snow Lodge at Old Faithful. A snug, modest accommodation, it is kept open every winter and is operated by the Yellowstone Park Company. Snow Lodge is also the only winter accommodation inside the park.

Once you are based at Snow Lodge, there are a number of options. A few minutes' ski run (or slightly longer on snowshoes) will take a person past Old Faithful to the Firehole River, along which bands of elk will certainly be encountered. They are used to visitors and do not pay a lot of attention to camera-wielding skiers. In a half day's tour, a skier will be able to focus on many elk and possibly a few mule deer and bison within a mile or two of the glowing fireplace at Snow Lodge.

A day's trip, on which you carry lunch, downstream along the Firehole, will reveal scenes of

fantastic steamy beauty. Lodgepole pines laden
with frost loom as ghosts along the trail, with
more elk wandering about them. Herds of buffalo
also will materialize in the distance. An alternative is to ride out on the snow coach in the morning for a drop-off somewhere and then ski back
to Snow Lodge. Or take one of the overnight ski
camping trips arranged on a regular basis and
guided by professionals.

Every winter many visitors spend a few days
around Old Faithful without ever clamping on a
ski or snowshoe. But they're missing a great deal,
because both can be rented there. The best advice, though, is to take your own. There is plenty
of room to carry all your gear on the snow
cruisers, and it is certainly more economical.

Incidentally, our duffel bag always includes
warmer clothing than a person might require in
normal ski touring elsewhere: for instance, two
pairs of longjohns apiece instead of just one.
Yellowstone winter temperatures drop to rock
bottom, and there are whole days when the mercury may never rise above zero. Add to this the
fact that a photographer stops frequently in his
running to shoot, and the need for warmer garments topside is more apparent. Bring warmest
mittens. Maybe even with handwarmers hidden
inside.

A camera hunter in winter or any other time
needs a camera system that permits the use of
telephoto lenses. The best kind of camera to
carry on skis, by far, is the 35mm single-lens
reflex—usually called the 35 SLR. This is com-
pact, easy and fast to operate, and lighter in
weight than all others (except the minis). It is
rugged enough to withstand rough use and handling and is the easiest to use with telephoto
lenses.

Depending on how you look at it, telephoto
lenses either magnify the size of the target in the
viewfinder—or bring the target closer to the
shooter. Next to bad exposures, too-small wildlife
subjects (in the pictures) are the greatest disap-
pointments of camera shooters. Besides getting as
close as possible or practicable to a bird or animal, you must narrow the gap, usually, even
more with a telephoto. Many of the best wildlife
pictures are those in which the animal is most
prominent and shown in greatest detail of fur and
feathers, antlers, snow flurries on the back, and
even highlights in the eyes.

The sight of a whitetail bounding away is common
for eastern skiers. Keep a camera handy and try to
get shots like this. ERWIN A. BAUER.

Mule deer bucks pause to look back at the author
long enough for this picture before bounding away
over a hillside deep in snow. ERWIN A. BAUER.

Moose are among the most co-operative of wildlife subjects for cameramen. But rarely is it possible to approach as near as the author's wife, Peggy, in these photos. Winter and skis make the difference. ERWIN A. BAUER.

Moose are among the most expressive animals a photographer can find. ERWIN A. BAUER.

But what telephoto should a ski cameraman use? Between us, Peggy and I always carry along a 500mm mirror (or reflex) lens to fit the pair of 35 SLRs in our rucksacks. That 500mm gives 10-power magnification, which is a boon at times. But I would rather not use it, preferring instead an old standby 200mm telephoto that is only 4-power. When it is hand-held on skis, there is too much chance (with the 500mm) for human error in focusing and movement (the latter especially in a wind), and the result is blurring or indistinct results. Besides, the usefulness of the 500mm lens with a fixed f/stop (at f8) is limited in poor light. So I try to get as close to my quarry as possible and hope the 200mm will be adequate. In places such as Yellowstone, it is. I may even be able to turn to a shorter lens, such as the 135mm.

Zoom lenses, which give a photographer magnification ranging from three or four power to twice that, are widely available. Most of them are excellent and convenient for a camera hunter on skis. The main drawbacks would be in size (bulk) and weight. And snow must be kept out of the moving parts. It is an individual matter to decide whether one heavy outfit is better to lug along than two or three, each of which is lighter.

I carry camera and telephotos alike in a nylon compartmented rucksack, which has been waterproofed around the seams. If there is any chance at all of a wet snow or rain, I wrap each piece individually in a plastic waterproof bag. Moisture is something to be kept out of all photo equipment at all costs. If droplets get inside—and freeze there—forget about shooting wildlife.

It is probably safe enough for a skilled skier to carry a camera hung around his neck, especially if it is encased. But that way it isn't any more ready to use than when it is inside a rucksack. Also, a camera with a long telephoto attached is a genuine nuisance dangling around the neck unless there are frequent needs for it. It can even be dangerous in case of a sudden spill. Most of the time a skier will spot a wildlife target from a distance rather than stumble upon it suddenly, and there will be time to get set up to shoot.

We find many of our subjects when we are driving by car. Assume that a bull moose is spotted a half mile or so from the road (such long-range spotting of wildlife is more possible against a white background); we park at the nearest widening and there clamp on either skis or the snowshoes that are always handy. Then we go out on foot, or rather on skis or snowshoes.

Much of the literature on wildlife photography advises hunters to use stealth—the same hidden approach that gun hunters would use—when stalking a trophy. That theory is bunk. From our own experience (and not only on skis and snowshoes), the odds favor a cameraman who makes every effort to stay out in the open, always within view of his target. A lot of animals simply are less wary of something strange that they can keep an eye on than of something that tries to sneak up and surprise them. We've found that to come up suddenly on even one of our "tame" neighborhood moose will send it shuffling off toward Idaho.

Still, there are some tricks to approaching game. Never ski directly toward a relaxed or undisturbed animal. Instead go obliquely, changing direction, pausing often, especially at any signs of nervousness. Each time you narrow the gap, shoot a picture in case you approach no closer. With experience you learn that certain flicks of the tail, or some sounds, or the behavior of one animal in a herd is a sign of uneasiness. Then slow down even more. Take your time.

Try not to keep staring or focusing directly for very long at any except those rare animals entirely familiar with human presence. On the other hand, keep looking away so as to seem uninterested. An animal that keeps grazing, looking up at you only occasionally, isn't overly frightened. I've never known a large animal to behave aggressively—to charge—during midwinter, but do not write off the possibility if an animal is "pushed" too far by a cameraman.

The greatest satisfactions—as well as the finest results—come from starting out on skis across a sparkling winter landscape. If it is near home and familiar, we already know in which direction to aim and most likely find something to film. If we do not know the place well, we probably will choose to parallel a stream or open waterway that bisects or is close to evergreen cover. As any veteran outdoorsman knows, there is much to be learned from the signs that wildlife leaves behind in the snow.

Tracks are the most evident, and a multitude of them means that animals are somewhere nearby. Learn which animals the tracks belong to. If they are fresh enough they can be followed to a conclusion—and a picture. There is a lot of excitement and suspense in this kind of trailing. But a knowledge of which tracks are fresh (or how fresh they are) and which are not fresh is very important. It can mean the difference between a wild goose chase and a roll full of fine exposures. In time, deeply etched tracks will tell you how fast or slow an animal is traveling—and therefore what your chances are of catching up. The way to be completely assured that tracks are fresh is to ski out after a new snowfall. But tracks are not the only telltale signs. Various droppings reveal wildlife occupancy of a place. Watch also where willow, balsam, alder, and other browse plants have been nipped off. Some wildlife will clear snow away by pawing and digging with hoofs.

There are scattered places where wildlife is attracted by winter feeding—by Good Samaritan handouts from man to help get them through the winter. Obviously these are good places to go camera hunting on skis. Find where they are.

Weather can be an important factor in finding wildlife. On days when it is abnormally cold and windy, we tour the trails that wind through tall timber, both for our own comfort and because we expect to find wildlife using the same shelter. Although wildlife may not be too active on very still, bright days, many species will emerge into the open to soak up welcome sunshine—and that's where we go hunting.

Not every day afield produces pictures suitable for publication—or anything at all worthwhile. But other days have been bonanzas when everything has worked out well—when all wildlife seemed to be posing and performing in a scenic winter setting. But fair weather or foul, we have rarely failed to find something of interest. Tracks often have told interesting tales, as where an owl or a coyote captured a mouse. The icy slide resembling a miniature toboggan run has revealed where a family of otters has been playing at the edge of the Snake River only minutes before our arrival. More than once we have paused to watch a water ouzel—or dipper—that most remarkable nondescript bird that actually walks under water on the most bitter days of the season. Or how about the Canada jays and the pine grosbeak, which have suddenly and silently materialized from nowhere when we have sat down deep in a pine woods to enjoy a snack? The visit was so unexpected that we forgot to shoot pictures of the freeloaders.

As physical condition improves and confidence increases, a skier also becomes a keener wildlife observer just because he can concentrate on it more. Toward the conclusion of every season, we miss little as we glide along. It's sad to see the season end, because many months will pass before the hunting is so good again.

CHAPTER 10

SNOWSHOEING

The nearest sport to cross-country skiing—the one that is most similar in all aspects—is snowshoeing. Like touring, it is an exercise that carries one into the quiet winter outdoors where few others can venture. Snowshoeing is even easier to master than skiing, because you simply walk on webs, only with a slightly wider stance than on booted feet. Although, for me at least, there is much more exhilaration to skiing, there are many times when snowshoeing is far more practical.

BACKGROUND

Except in a few scattered northern communities, snowshoeing had become an all-but-forgotten art except by a handful of wilderness trappers, some forest rangers, and scattered natives of the Arctic not yet introduced to snowmobiles. But there was a time long ago when snowshoes were absolutely indispensable in northern latitudes. Some kind of foot extender was necessary to get around from place to place—in truth, just to survive in the least hospitable climate on earth. For a long time the snowshoe was a more important development than the wheel—in places where wheels still are largely useless.

The first snowshoes were merely foot extenders —devices that increased the size of a person's sole and thereby distributed his weight over a greater area of snow surface. Without such devices a man would sink hopelessly in soft snow;

with them he could walk on top, or at least not sink as deep. Snowshoes almost certainly reached the New World from Asia over the Bering Strait, either by a once-existent land "bridge" or over the ice pack. Somewhere in that murky past, the forerunner of the framed-webbed snowshoe we know today evolved.

Snowshoes were in use by Eskimos and even more so by Indians all over northern Canada and the United States when the first visitors from Europe arrived. Indians had unlimited material available for framing; Eskimos did not. New settlers and explorers from Maine to Kodiak Island adopted the idea and may have improved on it. A mystery remains, however: Why didn't Leif Ericson, the Norse explorer, make any mention of snowshoes in his otherwise detailed accounts? Ericson had arrived in the New World five centuries before the first arrivals from England.

The Indians who relied most on snowshoes were the widely separated Algonquins of America's Northeast and the Athapascans of the Pacific Northwest. But we know that Indians of the Great Plains also used snowshoes—less sophisticated ones—to some extent. The webs made it possible to approach to within point-blank bow-and-arrow range of buffaloes. In deep snows, the huge beasts became hopelessly bogged down, while their pursuers were not.

The basic pattern of the Indian snowshoe was roughly an egg- or oval-shaped wooden frame woven with animal thong in the gridwork manner of a tennis racket. Each group of Indians produced shoes best suited to their particular conditions of snow and terrain. Some tribes even used different snowshoes from season to season. The technique was to bend green saplings to the desired shape and weave the webbing out of hide from the same caribou, deer, or moose that was used as food. On even the crudest snowshoes, some Indians were probably far more mobile in winter than they would have been in the mosquito-infested swamps and dense woodlands of summer.

Snowshoes played a fairly prominent part in the French and Indian Wars of the 1700s, especially in one 1758 engagement near Lake George in the Adirondacks. Most records of that drawn-out guerrilla conflict still refer to the encounter as the Battle of the Snowshoes. Snowshoes seemed to prove so well the value of free maneuvering in midwinter that officials in the various colonies supplied their militiamen with snowshoe equipment. Even the British, who were then rejecting new ideas, caught the point and put some infantrymen on webs.

Beaver trappers who explored and opened up parts of the American West relied on snowshoes. Wintering in places such as Jackson Hole would otherwise have been out of the question. Ranchers in the same country still may use snowshoes (or skis) occasionally when they are the only way to reach and feed livestock trapped by terrible winter storms. The various expeditions organized by Peary, Franklin, Amundsen, Byrd, and others to reach the North and South poles included snowshoes in their planning, but by this time the age of the snowshoe was well past. Technology and internal-combustion engines, not taut webs crunching over cold snow, would conquer the ends of the earth.

Some of my older readers may recall how, during the early decades of this century, snowshoeing clubs were for a time popular in eastern Canada and northern New England. These fraternal groups boasted distinctive insignia, flags, flashy uniforms, mascots, brass bands, and drill teams. The memberships held regular outings, which they called expeditions, every winter. It was prestigious to be a card-carrying member—and surely more worthwhile than belonging to popular groups of the day that relied on secret rites rather than on healthful exercise to hold people together. The clubs survive now only in the archives of a less frantic past.

Snowshoeing has enjoyed a fresh surge of interest since the late sixties. It parallels the ski-touring boom but is more modest. Nowadays snowshoeing is a quiet and contemplative sport—strictly ungregarious and unclublike. If today's most serious snowshoers join anything at all, it will be the Sierra Club, the Wilderness Society, or some hard-core environmental-action committee. Bravo for that!

But how does snowshoeing differ from skiing? Which is better? And why? There isn't any single answer. Personal preference, temperature, snow conditions, and the mission are what make all the difference.

During any winter season, Peggy and I do both, and there are others in that same category. Snowshoeing is best in a situation where a skier might sink hopelessly—as when a heavy new snowfall remains unbroken and uncompacted. Skiing is definitely best after some compaction has taken place or when there is a track to follow. Being often engaged in wildlife photography, we also find many instances when snowshoes provide a firmer base than skis for shooting nervous or moving animals. For that reason we carry skis and snowshoes all winter in our station wagon.

Heavier loads can be carried in greater safety for longer distances on snowshoes than on standard touring skis. Progress is slower, however, because great speed just isn't possible on webs. A number of times during late big-game-hunting seasons, I have helped to pack quarters of meat from the kill site to the handiest road on snowshoes. I would not have wanted to do it on skis.

This isn't to say that heavy loads cannot be toted on skis, but snowshoes do make the job more sure. Snowshoeing is a dependable rather than a swift means of cross-country. It may even require more effort per mile, burning up more calories, unless the snowshoer maintains the deliberately slow and steady pace that is absolutely the best. There is always a strong temptation to hurry. Resist it, because on webs you will tire too quickly.

Initially, snowshoeing is easy to master. But it does take getting used to. Those large, unfamiliar frames can trip up a person in the beginning, and a lot of new leg and thigh muscles are called into play. But a person who can stand up on two feet can also stand up on snowshoes. Maintaining balance isn't difficult at all. Almost anyone can start snowshoeing the day he first straps the webs onto his boots.

EQUIPMENT

Equipment for snowshoeing is even simpler and less expensive than for ski touring, because an outdoorsman may already own all he needs except the snowshoes and bindings. Big-game-hunting clothing and the cross-country skiing garments already described will be more than adequate. No special boots are necessary; a snowshoer can wear any boots that have already proved comfortable and warm enough for other winter activities.

The selection of serviceable snowshoes can be bewildering, but mostly on account of nomenclature. The basic design hasn't changed in centuries, and today a buyer pays more for craftsmanship than for any new advances in design—with one exception to be considered later. The confusing fact is that shoes are sold as bearpaws, Michigans, Maines, cross-countries, Green Mountains, Adirondacks, guides, rangers, trappers, tear drops, Alaskans, Labradors, and probably more than any committee could tabulate here. But any two or more of these varieties probably are the same or so similar that not even a snowshoe maker could tell them apart. The name too often depends on the manufacturer's whim or the place of origin, rather than on any distinctive design. Let's try to simplify as much as possible.

The most commonly used and most traditional framing for snowshoes is some kind of straight-grained, strong-fibered, pliable wood. New England white ash fits the specifications very well. Besides, it grows handy to where most of the wood-frame snowshoes originate today. Stiffness in a frame is very desirable, and consequently aluminum-tubing frames have recently entered the picture.

Except for nylon rope that is woven on some cheap shoes, webbing today is made either of rawhide thong or of neoprene, a synthetic. The latter material may not appeal to traditionalists as much as rawhide, but it does have some advantages. Neoprene is lighter than leather, and leather stretches when wet. Neoprene is rodent-proof, and it is impervious to petroleum products, which can ruin leather. Since many snowshoes are stored away in garages and barns, a lot of thong webbing is consumed by spilled oil, grease,

Snowshoes are often handy—perhaps even essential—around late-season hunting camps, such as this one on Michigan's Upper Peninsula. ERWIN A. BAUER.

Good snowshoes can carry a man across deep, soft, new snowfalls that would be impassable on foot alone. UTAH TRAVEL COUNCIL.

rats, mice, porcupines, and even man's best friend. Neoprene also seems to resist wet snow buildup better than leather.

The consensus is that short, broad shoes (by *any* of the names I have listed) are best for woods and brushy trails because they are easiest to maneuver. Similarly, the longer, narrower shoes are usually chosen for best going across the open. Webbing should also be "tighter"—the grid strips closer together—for soft and fluffy snow conditions. But personal preference should also be a factor, and a beginner should try to sample different styles and shapes where he will use them most. I find it easier to travel anywhere in the thinner (narrower) shoes, because possibly my legs are not quite so widespread during stride. But I know other snowshoers who feel exactly the opposite.

Still, the single, main consideration is for a shoe with sufficient undersurface to support the wearer's weight over the snow. The closer it is possible to attain the ideal size, the better. Snowshoes that are too large will be heavier than necessary and will increase fatigue. Too small a shoe is also an unfortunate waste of energy, because it will allow a man to sink too far with each step. I know of no way, no chart, no scale guaranteed to pin down accurately the proper size of snowshoe for every person.

The catalogs of most snowshoe manufacturers are of some basic assistance, however. Their charts compare persons of different weights with shoes of various designs and sizes. They also include helpful hints about the selection of shapes for regional use. If it proves impossible to try out various shapes and sizes before buying, the catalog is probably the second best place to begin.

Now let's look at snowshoes a little more closely to understand their use. The main part of any serviceable, modern snowshoe is a crosspiece in the framing that is just forward of the balance center of the shoe. There is also an open space five or six inches square in the webbing just in front of this crosspiece. The ball of the snowshoer's foot sits directly on top of the crossmember and actually pivots there. As he walks, his toe dips down into the opening and back up again. As in cross-country skiing, the heel is unattached to the ski and remains free.

Look at it another way. When the foot is raised for each step forward, the snowshoe binding per-

Traditional snowshoes with design generally unchanged for centuries have wooden frames and rawhide thong webbing. ERWIN A. BAUER.

mits the tail of the snowshoe to drop down. At the same time, the snowshoe toe flips up. Any good binding should permit this—and never restrict the motion, which is really that of walking normally.

An ideal binding has two purposes. First, it should hold the boot in place securely, with no slack either from side to side or from front to rear. At the same time, it should hinge up and down to about forty-five degrees when the snowshoe is lifted well off the ground. It is especially vital that the boot be held in place over the crossbar when the snowshoe is going downhill, and frequent adjustments should not be necessary. Second, any good binding should be easy to buckle or attach to the boot, an especially critical feature when hands are numb with cold. Thousands of kinds of bindings have been invented and widely used. The best, most efficient ones feature some kind of "stirrup" into which the boot toe is placed directly over the crossbar. A strap or two around and behind the boot holds it in place.

The most important change in snowshoe design in generations is seen in these Sherpa models, with aluminum tube framing and neoprene webbing. ERWIN A. BAUER.

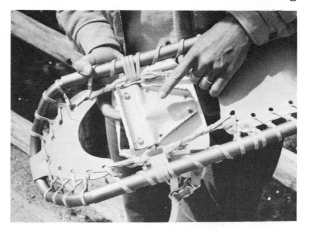

Details of underside of Sherpa snowshoe; note hinged, sawtoothed part, which is bound onto the boot. ERWIN A. BAUER.

Some snowshoes have long tails, turned-up tips, or both. Maybe the long tail was once meant as a rudder, which (as it dragged) kept the shoe pointed straight ahead. That could compensate somewhat for a loose or inefficient binding, but the tail shouldn't be necessary. The turned-up tip helps to prevent digging into soft snow with each step forward, which a flat tip might do. Even small amounts of snow soon make a labor of walking, and a snowshoer gets the idea that he is shoveling a path rather than snowshoeing on one. For me the greatest advantage in curved-up tips has been in the safety of going downhill. Naturally, the curved-up tips are more expensive.

A NEW DEPARTURE

The farther any person travels on snowshoes, the heavier the shoes seem to be and the greater the fatigue. The first really significant breakthrough in lighter snowshoes was made recently by Bill and Barbara Prater of Tacoma, Washington, who have developed and are selling shoes with aluminum-tube frames. Their Sherpa snowshoes are revolutionary in design and are much more efficient than the traditional wood-frame shoes for most cross-snow travel.

Besides the aluminum frames, the crosspiece is a steel-plated hinge (with nylon bushing to pro-

tect against wear) built into the snowshoe frame. With the binding attached so that the ball of the foot rests squarely atop the hinge rod, free and smooth forward motion is assured as the snowshoe flops freely up and down. For the first time ever, the Praters claim, perfect parallel tracking on the trail is possible. There is no side-to-side flipflopping of the shoe. Our own testing in various conditions confirms that.

Much more is new, different, and improved with the Sherpa shoes. Serrated metal edges—teeth—on the bottoms of the bindings provide a built-in traction system. One weakness of the traditional snowshoes is that they do not grip well on hardened or icy surfaces, especially in climbing, but this metal grip certainly changes all that.

Even the webbings have been altered on the Sherpa shoes. Neoprene decking has been substituted for the crisscrossed rawhide thongs. At first we thought that this might collect snow, but we soon discovered that snow doesn't stick to the neoprene at all—not even very wet snow. That decking feature, plus the lighter aluminum frames, has made it possible for smaller (and lighter) shoes of the Sherpa design to support the same weight as a larger shoe of traditional design.

As I write this chapter, the Sherpa snowshoes we've used have been maintenance free and take up little space among the outdoor gear carried all winter long in our station wagon. Perhaps for the first time since solid wood slats gave way to wood-framed, webbed shoes centuries ago, there has been a radical advance in snowshoe design.

Sherpa snowshoes can help a hunter climb in country even as steep as this. ERWIN A. BAUER.

The Sherpa types are probably the working snowshoes of the foreseeable future, especially in the mountainous country to which they are especially suited.

Some snowshoers prefer ski poles; others succeed well without them. A few depend on one pole as balance insurance. The same length of pole recommended for cross-country skiing is best; however, it might be stiffer, because it will not be used to propel a person forward on the trail. If there is a choice, the basket for snowshoeing should be about six inches in diameter. I have encountered some snowshoers, who climb, employing an ice ax instead of a ski pole, but with a basket attached just above the point end. I have seen still another snow traveler with a screw mounting placed on the handle of his ski pole so that he could use it as a monopod for his camera. It's an idea well worth copying by other photographers.

Special boots such as are needed for ski touring are not necessary for snowshoeing. It's better to use whatever winter footgear has already proved comfortable and warm. I like to wear the same twelve-inch boot pacs (leather tops, rubber bottoms, with felt inner soles) that I wear for most

late-fall hunting. But I have also used lower (ten-inch) all-leather bird-shooter boots for short hikes when there was no snow thaw. With these and with any other low boots, it is a good idea to wear gaiters (as described for skiing) to keep snow from sifting down into the tops.

Especially with new "stiff" leather or neoprene, bindings should first be carefully matched to fit the boots. Set the boot exactly in the right place on top of the snowshoe on a bare floor. Next, tighten all the straps to achieve a snug fit. It may be necessary to adjust them once or twice after a short hike, but after that the bindings should always fit well as long as the same boots are used.

HOW TO USE SNOWSHOES

It's possible to get the knack of snowshoeing before snow ever falls. If you don't mind the smirks of neighbors, put them on in the backyard (or else on grass sod) and just walk around. That way you quickly learn the one aspect that is different from walking without webs: You must employ a wider stance, because it's impossible to walk while one snowshoe holds the other down. Pick up one foot and move it far enough ahead and over the other, never coming down on it— not even on a small corner of it. For some, this will require a longer stride and wider stance. But once you get the hang of it, and you will quickly, you will travel comfortably without ever thinking about the problem of tripping up. Otherwise snowshoeing on the level is just walking.

If practical, take the first steps on tramped-out or fairly compacted snow. Next, try it in deeper and deeper snow; you probably will be surprised that you do not sink. If the snowshoes do not have turned-up tips, you might have to make a conscious effort in the beginning to put down heels first as you walk. First-timers should also be given the benefit (when possible) of following another snowshoer rather than breaking his own trail. But stop right here to check and tighten bindings if a toe is pinched or everything doesn't seem completely comfortable. If you are using ski poles, move the right one ahead as you move the left foot and vice versa, but do not thrust hard with the arms as when skiing. Use the poles for balance until, perhaps, you find them unnecessary.

To be sure, you might step on one snowshoe with the other and fall down in a snowbank. A pole or two will help you to get upright again if no one else is there to lend a hand. Use the poles as levers. Lacking poles or a companion, try to draw your legs and shoes under you before standing up. It may be necessary to remove the snowshoes, and that's where a simple buckle binding comes in handiest.

As soon as snowshoeing over a flat surface becomes second nature, look for slopes. You'll discover that most of them are no more difficult to negotiate than level surfaces. If they are, try angling up rather than going straight up. If it is a very long slope, go by switchbacking—traversing —by taking a diagonal Z-shaped trail up the hill. Another technique for very short, steep places is by sidestepping as described for skiers. When bindings fit and are secure, almost any hillside can be conquered by carefully selecting the route ahead, taking advantage of the most gentle gradients. A little experience will help a lot.

Turning is done almost exactly as skiers do it, except that, snowshoes being shorter, it is easier. Make any change of direction by the step/turn method, always being careful not to plant one web on the other, with legs wide apart.

Downhill slopes, particularly steep or icy ones, can present problems and should be approached with caution by beginners. In such spots it is too easy to find yourself suddenly upside down in a heap of snow at the bottom. Always go diagonally rather than straight down unless the bindings are absolutely secure and fitted onto the boots. Otherwise a toe could dig down into the snow and cause a headlong pitch forward. When fairly hard snow covers a moderate slope, it may be possible to sit down on the snowshoes and reach the bottom by tobogganing. But the teeth of the new Sherpa shoes I described take a lot of the uncertainty out of any slope.

With soft or new snow conditions, even the snowshoes best matched to the snowshoer will sink down to some extent with each step. There is also a natural tendency to hurry one's pace, to avoid the sinking. Resist this urge, because it is unduly tiring. Instead, walk deliberately, pausing ever so briefly after putting down each foot,

Snowshoes are a symbol of winter and deep snows in the North, even when cached in a snowbank against a January sunset. ERWIN A. BAUER.

rather than trying to tread lightly in the hope of not sinking in. This slight pause causes snow underfoot to change structure, compacting and becoming a firmer launch pad for the next step.

The second snowshoer in a file has much easier going than the first over new snow. The third has still easier going, and so on. To give everyone an even break and forestall fatigue, rotate regularly the chore of trail-breaking.

It is a very hard thing to describe, but with practice a snowshoer can achieve the same rolling gait with which Indian snowshoers and trappers can cover long distances without tiring. The entire body shifts weight from side to side and in a motion not unlike the rhythmic paddling of a canoe. The emphasis should be on steadiness, in keeping on the move while "leaning" ahead, but never on hurrying.

Snowshoeing is a splendid physical conditioner and as safe and steady a means for crossing deep snow as man has yet devised. But it's also an excellent way to enjoy nature in a wintry mood. Along with ski touring it's a far finer tranquilizer than any drugs a doctor might prescribe for tension or cabin fever.

Even when they are hanging up, retired from use forever inside a weathered barn, snowshoes have a magic and a beauty that stored golf clubs or any other athletic gear cannot possibly match. Nor is there anything exactly like the unique overlapping tracks of snowshoes on snow leading to some distant destination and adventure.

CHAPTER 11

COPING WITH WINTER EMERGENCIES

From a ski tourer's standpoint, the essence of coping with winter—of staying safe and comfortable on the trail—is always to conserve body heat and energy. The aim should always be to maintain heat, and not overheat; to maintain an energy reserve, an ability to conclude an adventure safely. Travel at a steady pace—your *own* steady pace, at the speed you can maintain without undue effort, and you will never get into trouble.

Most cross-country touring is done in small groups or parties, and the element of competition is bound to pop up. Well and good, but do not push yourself unduly. The leader of a party should see that all travel goes at the same steady pace that the slowest person can maintain without struggling. Better yet, parties should be segregated so that skiers of similar ability and endurance are grouped.

Whenever a party is breaking a new trail over unbroken snow, or traveling over an old trail that has been drifted, the first skier invariably has the hardest task—and it becomes easier the farther back one skis in the line. But this is no place for iron-man stunts. Leadership in breaking trail should be alternated, with everyone taking turns. If a picnic lunch is being carried, everyone should alternate in lugging the load.

It is always a good idea to pause often, not only for a breather, but also to enjoy winter's beauty better. These stops are also an opportunity to adjust equipment. If boots or bindings begin to rub or pinch, if bindings need adjustment, as they might, these problems should be corrected immediately. Laces or straps that are tied too tightly, folds in a sock, or loose gaiters can be irritating and cause blisters. Any raw, red, or scraped spots on the feet should be taped or bandaged as soon as they are discovered. If the traveling seems particularly burdensome—labored and slow—to anyone, it's possible that the skis have not been properly waxed. Take time to correct this. As curious as it may seem, scraping off old wax and replacing it with a proper application can even solve some uncomfortable foot and boot problems.

As far as possible, especially when you are embarking on a longer trip, do not allow yourself or anyone else to sweat so profusely as to soak all your clothing. In the exuberance of starting a high adventure, that's an easy thing to do. You push ahead too aggressively, with uncomfortable consequences later. Keep clothing dry. In the case of rain or a wet snow falling, add foul-weather gear before you really need it. Then slow down so that you do not sweat too much underneath it.

A good rule of thumb is never to venture farther on any trip—be it for one day or several—than you can ski back easily on your own ability and energy. For most people, enjoyment is the entire reason for cross-country skiing, and there is no use in inviting trouble. If you are unusually fatigued, do not be ashamed to turn back sooner than planned. Always watch the weather, which in winter and especially in mountain areas can change rapidly, even savagely. Sudden high winds are often an indication. So are dense banks of clouds spilling over mountains into the valleys below. Deteriorating weather can create problems in getting back to a starting point. Low clouds

No skier should go beyond the point where he has grave doubts about returning. To keep from getting lost, follow your own tracks to the starting place. ONTARIO MINISTRY OF INDUSTRY AND TOURISM.

Stop often for breathers or for making adjustments in equipment. Easier going on the trail might be as simple as rewaxing the skis. UTAH TRAVEL COUNCIL.

can quickly obscure landmarks on which a skier depends. Unexpected winds can cover up trails at the same time that they sap the body heat on which a skier depends.

It is a matter of record that most accidents— mishaps of all sorts—occur after skiers become tired, hungry, too cold, and probably too wet. All at once there is the inclination to take shortcuts, to tackle steeper hills than is wise, to press faster and faster to reach a warm, secure place. A wise ski tourer should resist the temptations. Return to the starting base the safest, surest way, even if it takes longer. Most of all, keep warm by avoiding perspiration and keeping clothes dry. Avoiding heat loss is the best advice anyone can give a cross-country skier.

HEAT LOSS

Heat loss happens in a number of ways, all controllable: by radiation, conduction, convection, evaporation, respiration, water chill, and wind chill. Radiation is usually the chief cause of heat loss among ski tourers, and it emphasizes the need for proper rather than stylish clothing. Remember the advice about layers in Chapter 2. Consider, for example, how not wearing a cap can gradually sacrifice up to half of a body's total heat at forty degrees Fahrenheit. It is therefore true that cold feet and hands can be somewhat warmed by adding headgear.

Prolonged contact with anything colder than the skin temperature leads to loss of body heat by conduction. Therefore do not sit or lie down in snow or on frozen ground, no matter how tired you are. The longer you so relax, the stiffer and more chilled you will become, and the harder it will be to warm up again.

In Chapter 2 I said that the main function of skiing garments was to retain a layer of radiated warm air close to the skier's body—to assure the normal 98.6 degrees of body temperature. Cooler air passing or brushing the body tends to remove warmth (warm air) by convection. The blowing of the wind is one kind of convection, and so is racing downhill at a high speed. The faster this

During intense cold, there can be great heat loss through respiration. A face mask like this can reduce much of the heat loss. ERWIN A. BAUER.

exchange of air, the greater the heat loss. As wind velocity increases and moderate body temperatures become more difficult to maintain, add more clothing or provide other shelter for the body.

Warmth is also dissipated just by breathing, by inhaling cold air. In extreme cold—say, subzero —this heat loss can be reduced by breathing through a scarf, handkerchief, or cotton mask- made for the purpose. Evaporation of sweat is another kind of heat loss, and water chill is even worse. Keep firmly in mind that wet clothing can extract vital heat from the body at a rate several times faster than dry clothing. One fabric, wool, as pointed out earlier, remains warmer than other fabrics when it is wet. Nevertheless, keep wool garments dry, too, by never skiing so vigorously that you overheat.

ENERGY CONSERVATION

Any skier's available supply of energy is limited, and he can go only so far on additional energy intake. In other words, it's as necessary to conserve energy as it is warmth, and invariably the two depend upon each other.

We know that it requires (on the average) about seventeen hundred calories to sustain a person comfortably at rest for about twenty-four hours. But, depending on how severe the weather and the type of terrain to cross, a Nordic skier can use up five thousand or six thousand calories in one day's touring. Strenuous exercise expends calories rapidly, for it also produces heat. Obviously the calories must be continually replaced. That means that a skier must remain on a nourishing and well-balanced diet while he is active in the skiing season.

In the field, a ski tourer also should carry along enough high-energy snacks to replace lost calories (energy, body heat). It's both wise and pleasant to pause for five-minute breaks to enjoy a snack. Such breaks also are of just the right duration to get rid of some of the lactic acid buildup in muscles, which is a result of great exertion.

As any winter outdoor sports fan knows, the same high-calorie foods that are best for restoring energy are also the most delicious. Some examples are chocolate, cashews, pecans, almonds, peanuts, macadamia nuts, dried fruits, congealed (frozen or sugared) honey or maple syrup, and unrefined brown cane sugar. Various mixtures of these ingredients, called gorp, are packaged and sold in most ski and mountain shops. But anyone can concoct his own formula at home for a fraction of the cost.

An important point should be inserted here. Alcohol in any form is a depressant and never a heat or energy builder. The goatskin bag of wine is something a wise skier should skip. If alcoholic beverages have a place in skiing, it is at the end of the day, or the end of a trip, off the trails and in a warm haven somewhere. To put it as bluntly as possible, drinking has resulted in serious cross-country skiing accidents, including too many fatalities.

Every active ski tourer loses a good bit of moisture through perspiration, breathing, and urination, and it must be replaced by drinking fluids. Three or four quarts daily may not be too much to prevent dehydration—if the skiing is very strenuous. Water can be retained in the body much longer if there is salt in the gorp or if salt tablets are taken. Some medical authorities disagree about the true value of such salt supplements; they do not disagree, however, on the need for drinking plenty of water before starting out on a tour and at the end of it.

Some veteran skiers, especially racers, train to do without water during a tour or a run. They also devoutly avoid any temptation to eat snow, a temporary thirst quencher that soon makes matters seem worse—more or less, depending on the amount of pollution. But many people must have water to enjoy a trip genuinely, and there is nothing wrong with it. If pure, unfrozen surface water isn't available along the way, carry along a supply in an aluminum canteen. Add sugared or fruit flavoring if you like, but keep in mind that this may increase your thirst.

GETTING LOST

While the odds of getting lost are low, it is a possibility that cannot be ignored. It is the most common emergency of all, and every skier should be mentally prepared to cope with it. Usually it amounts to no more than briefly losing your bearings and/or the trail—in other words, not knowing exactly where you are. It's seldom very serious if the skier will stop, sit down in a dry spot somewhere, and think over the matter. If several skiers are lost together, they should all stay together and discuss the situation. Do not separate. To panic or to act hastily, frantically, is to be avoided at all costs. Relax.

It is easy (even without a map and compass, which someone *should* have brought along) to determine the general direction. For this you need a pocket watch or wristwatch, and at least enough sunlight to make a shadow, even a weak one. Hold a match or straight twig upright at the edge of the watch face. Rotate the watch until the

Getting caught out sometime in a blizzard or wet snow is almost inevitable. Find shelter and stay dry. ERWIN A. BAUER.

shadow of the stick falls directly on the hour hand, no matter what the hour. Halfway between the hour hand and twelve points is due south. Exactly opposite is north. And so on.

Of course, the sun may not be visible at all, and even if you have wandered off a trail, probably it will be possible to follow (retreat) your own back track. If this has been obliterated by windblown snow, watch for tree blazes, snowpoles, or cairns; these would be visible well above the highest snow levels along frequently used trails in national parks and forests. A blaze is a distinctive slash mark cut or chopped into the bark of a tree to mark a route; blazes normally are placed at spots where a trail changes direction. On the best-marked trails, they are also placed so that the next blaze can be seen from any one blaze. In some parks and forests, splashes of fluorescent orange paint sprayed on tree trunks are substituted for slash marks in the bark. Before starting out on any long trips where there might be some question about the location of trails, ask about the system of blazing at park headquarters or at a ranger station. Remember that the directional signs so helpful to summertime hikers may be covered over by deep snow.

SO YOU'RE REALLY LOST

Let's assume that it is getting dark and your group has lost its way. The sun creates no shadow, and knowing your direction still wouldn't help. No familiar landmarks can be spotted anywhere. There are no blaze marks of any kind in evidence, and wind-driven snow has covered over your back tracks. The only wise choice is to siwash out—to make yourselves as comfortable as possible while you spend the night in the woods. If there is a cabin or any kind of crude shelter nearby, go to it.

To continue farther might only complicate the situation and make it more serious. It is too easy to blunder into trouble in the dark and even easier to use up precious heat and energy reserves. Morning may bring better light and recognition of your location. And a rescue party will have an easier time finding you if you do not wander away. You should have left some word of your plans behind, in case you did not return on schedule.

The first step is to select as sheltered an overnight place as possible—out of the full force of

Especially when you are backpacking (which can be hard work), you should avoid overheating or overexertion. Both leave you more susceptible to cold and hypothermia.
ERWIN A. BAUER.

the wind. Slowly collect as much firewood as you can and then some. Pile it up where it will be handy. Do this calmly, and by all means avoid sweating. Collect enough evergreen boughs as insulation on which to sit or lie down, perhaps even enough to construct a lean-to shelter or heat shield for the fire, or a windbreak. You may very well be able to find an area with many deadfalls, and these can be used both as shelter and as firewood. Put on all the clothes you have. Now light a fire and keep it going all night long; it will keep you warm, and the blaze or smoke might attract attention. Avoid a huge blazing fire that burns up wood too fast; concentrate rather on a smaller, hotter, smokeless fire around which you can all huddle. Above all, keep calm.

It is impossible in a plight such as this not to know fear and apprehension, particularly if you are not experienced in the wilderness. But it's probably far more uncomfortable than it is dangerous. Nowadays few if any cross-country skiers are ever lost—or even missing for very long—if they avoid panic. Everywhere in snow country today there are sophisticated rescue facilities and professional rescue patrols. Their record for finding lost souls in the toughest predicaments is amazingly good.

COLD CAN KILL

Still—and this warning must in good conscience be made—cold can kill. Every skier who ever ventures far from beaten paths must understand the chemistry of cold, as well as the fatigue, exhaustion, and psychology that go with it.

When you are traveling on skis—or doing any similar physical exercise—you begin to use up and gradually lose body heat. To counteract this, you exercise more vigorously to stay warm, or you add more clothing, or both. In addition, your body may make its own involuntary adjustments to preserve normal temperatures in vital organs. Either way, energy reserves—body heat—will in time drain away if you do not stop to rest and refuel. If the exposure (heat loss) continues (in the extreme) until energy reserves are exhausted, cold eventually reaches the brain. Then the skier begins to lose judgment without realizing it. As internal temperatures begin sliding too far downward, physical control is also gradually lost, perhaps first in the arms and legs, but again without the skier's really being aware of it. This state of exposure has a name: hypothermia. When body temperatures dip to ninety degrees Fahrenheit and below, the trend leads to stupor, collapse, and then death.

A wise ski tourer, however, need never reach a degree of exposure even bordering on hypothermia. Consider, for instance, how Eskimos have survived for countless centuries in the most terrible winters known. They did so mainly by remaining inactive indoors and by staying out of the most severe wind. A skier can do the same thing in less severe conditions by dressing adequately, by not overheating, by staying dry, and by avoiding the wind.

Unlikely as it might seem, most cases of hypothermia today occur in air temperatures between 20 and 50 degrees Fahrenheit, not in subzero temperatures. Perhaps many outdoorsmen simply cannot expect any danger in such moderate temperatures, and so they sometimes fatally underestimate what can happen. Therefore, if a skier cannot stay dry and warm under whatever weather conditions, using what clothing is available, he should terminate exposure. Get out of wind, cold, or rain the fastest way possible. Get dried out. If that isn't easily possible, give up whatever goal or destination was in mind. Find heat or build a fire and sit close to it. Calmly concentrate on getting dried out, because soaked clothing seriously refrigerates the body as the moisture evaporates.

Persistent or very violent shivering is a distinct warning of hypothermia to come. Never ignore it. Make camp or find warmth while a residue of energy still exists—and before you lose control of your situation.

It is far easier to spot the symptoms of hypothermia in others than in oneself. Whenever you are traveling in a party exposed to brutal wind, damp cold, rain, or wet snow, make it a policy for each skier to watch the others for such symptoms as uncontrollable, slurred, or unnatural speech, fumbling hands, lapses of memory, stumbling or lurching, and drowsiness. Difficulty in getting up or inability to do so after a rest are crucial signs that treatment is needed. A potential hypothermia victim may not even believe he is in trouble. But pay attention to the symptoms and not to the victim.

The most important step is to get any hypothermia victim out of wind and rain—indoors, if possible. There strip off all his wet clothes. If it is a mild case, give the skier warm, nonalcoholic drinks. Cocoa is great if it is handy. Or sugar water. Get the person into dry clothes and a warm sleeping bag. Wrapped warm rocks (never too hot) or a canteen of warm water slipped into the bag will help to warm an overexposed person.

If a person should lapse into semiconsciousness or worse, try to keep him awake while you supply warm drinks. Leave him stripped and put him into a warm sleeping bag along with another person, also stripped, who is in good health. If a double sleeping bag happens to be handy, put the victim between two stripped skiers, for the skin-to-skin contact is effective.

WIND-CHILL FACTOR

The aim should always be to prevent the onset of exhaustion and hypothermia. Individual tolerances to cold and exposure differ, because metabolisms differ. Individual psychology is another factor and one that cannot be measured. But how cold is *really* cold for *any* skier or snowshoer can be measured accurately by what is called the "wind-chill factor," now put into graphic form by the U.S. military services. The following wind-chill chart provides valuable information for cross-country skiers.

To use the chart properly, a skier needs to know the temperature and wind velocity. They can both be estimated closely enough for purposes of dressing properly to match the wind chill. It can be considered calm when bare trees stand motionless and chimney smoke rises vertically. At wind velocities below 12 mph, the smaller branches of trees will move, open water will be rippled, and you can feel the wind chill on exposed skin. From 12 to 25 mph larger tree branches will sway, wind will whistle in the branches, and snow will pile into drifts. Beyond 25 mph whole trees will bend and creak, snow drifting will become serious, and walking into the face of the wind will be difficult. So will skiing. Keep in mind that you can ski more open country on days when the wind-chill factor is low. You can save the trails through sheltered, forested country for the blustery occasions. No matter, though; the wind-chill chart is a good thing to carry in your wallet or belt pack on all skiing occasions.

WIND MPH (miles per hour)	TEMPERATURE (degrees Fahrenheit)																				
	40	35	30	25	20	15	10	5	0	−5	−10	−15	−20	−25	−30	−35	−40	−45	−50	−55	−60
	EQUIVALENT CHILL TEMPERATURE																				
5	35	30	25	20	15	10	5	0	−5	−10	−15	−20	−25	−30	−35	−40	−45	−50	−55	−60	−70
10	30	20	15	10	5	0	−10	−15	−20	−25	−35	−40	−45	−50	−60	−65	−70	−75	−80	−90	−95
15	25	15	10	0	−5	−10	−20	−25	−30	−40	−45	−50	−60	−65	−70	−80	−85	−90	−100	−105	−110
20	20	10	5	0	−10	−15	−25	−30	−35	−45	−50	−60	−65	−75	−80	−85	−95	−100	−110	−115	−120
25	15	10	0	−5	−15	−20	−30	−35	−45	−50	−60	−65	−75	−80	−90	−95	−105	−110	−120	−125	−135
30	10	5	0	−10	−20	−25	−30	−40	−50	−55	−65	−70	−80	−85	−95	−100	−110	−115	−125	−130	−140
35	10	5	−5	−10	−20	−30	−35	−40	−50	−60	−65	−75	−80	−90	−100	−105	−115	−120	−130	−135	−145
40	10	0	−5	−15	−20	−30	−35	−45	−55	−60	−70	−75	−85	−95	−100	−110	−115	−125	−130	−140	−150

WINDS ABOVE 40 MPH HAVE LITTLE ADDITIONAL EFFECT

LITTLE DANGER

INCREASING DANGER (flesh may freeze within one minute)

GREAT DANGER (flesh may freeze within 30 seconds)

AUTOMOBILE PREPARATION

Coping with winter and winter emergencies often begins before a skier tightens his bindings or waxes his skis. Just to reach a skiing area and to depart can cause problems, mostly automotive, and we might as well consider these here. The following is especially important to skiers who live in warmer latitudes and drive only occasionally into snow country for a holiday.

Consider first if the car tires are all suitable for snow travel. The treads should not be worn smooth, unless there are tire chains to make up for the lack of tread. Besides chains, winter travelers in deep-snow regions should also carry a shovel, ax, and tow chain or rope in the car. There should be enough antifreeze in the radiator to cope with subzero temperatures. One of the most widely overlooked, although critical, of all automotive items is the battery; it must be able to start the car when the engine is stiff and cold. A lot more battery power is required to turn over an engine when the mercury hovers at zero than when the weather is warm and balmy. Many people who live year 'round in skiing country carry jumper cables; these join two car batteries in series and enable one motorist to help another get started. Visitors might well carry jumpers, too.

Driving on snow and ice is neither difficult nor unsafe at sensible speeds, and so visitors traveling northward should allow sufficient time for the trip so that they can drive slowly. They might also

Park your vehicle so as to avoid drifting snow and to be able to drive away at the end of skiing. ERWIN A. BAUER.

keep advised of snow conditions (especially in mountainous areas) and expected storms through radio forecasts and state highway patrols.

Any RVs or campers, trailers, or cab-over pickups should be thoroughly winterized before going on a ski trip. Unless a permanent heat is maintained inside, all water tanks, toilets, and pipes must be completely drained to prevent freezing and bursting. It may also be a wise idea to insulate side panels and the camper roof to help hold heat inside. If the camper is self-contained be sure to park it where electrical plug-ins are handy.

Although the simple matter of parking may seem of no consequence, it's surely worth a few

When vehicle is in shape for winter, with all necessary equipment, there is no reason why a skiing holiday shouldn't be the happiest event of any winter. ERWIN A. BAUER.

If you are planning to use an RV or camper vehicle as ski headquarters on a skiing holiday, be sure that it is properly winterized for very cold weather. ERWIN A. BAUER.

When you are venturing far into deep-snow country, cars should be equipped for emergencies with shovels, chains, tow rope, and a fully charged, strong battery. ERWIN A. BAUER.

words here. Keep in mind that while you're off skiing, a restricted parking area near a trailhead can become wind-drifted with snow. Try to park where you will not have to dig out. Face the car toward your departure, with solid, unobstructed going straight ahead, downhill if possible, while the engine is still warm. Set it in low gear or park rather than using the handbrake, which on some older-model cars could freeze. In those autos (often pickups) where the battery is situated beneath the floorboards and is somewhat exposed, be certain that no slush or ice has accumulated on top of the terminals or around them. This can run down even a fresh, strong battery.

It is far better to hide car keys (in a place that all members of the party know about) somewhere near the car than to carry them in a pocket while you are ski touring across country. The chances of losing them that way are too great, and the chances of recovery in snow are nearly nil. It is also an excellent free form of "insurance" to stick a note in your windshield about your plans, destination, and estimated time of return. Park rangers and patrolmen will take note of it in case something goes wrong and you do not reappear.

For really long or extended skiing trips where temperatures are low, it may pay to have a hot-water-circulation heater installed on the engine block. In 1977 the cost of heater plus installation ran a little over $50. The heaters can be plugged overnight into any 110-volt outlet (conveniently placed outdoors at many motels and ski resorts) and will practically guarantee easy starting on the coldest mornings.

Use great caution when you are handling gasoline, because it is flammable and because it can contribute to the freezing of your hands. Gasoline (which can get much colder than the freezing point of water) can painfully, severely blister exposed skin. Bare hands can also become "frozen" to bare metal in subzero temperatures; wear gloves whenever you are making repairs or changing a tire. Coping with mechanical problems can cause more headaches on a skiing trip than anything else.

All things considered, coping with the worst possible winter—even in a wilderness or with a cranky automobile—is far safer than strolling on a city street nowadays after dark. There are statistics to prove that.

CHAPTER 12

AVALANCHE!

Everywhere in the world where snow piles high every winter, avalanches are almost certain to occur. Avalanches are slides, shifts, or rearrangements of snow accumulation that can amount to very little or can be highly dangerous, depending on the size. They can rank with floods, cyclones, earthquakes, and volcanic eruptions among nature's most terrible and destructive forces.

Also every year, avalanches claim the lives of many who spend time outdoors, and that would include some skiers and snowshoers. The number of ski and snowshoe victims is very small; a skier is far more likely to be injured when driving to ski country than he is while touring. Nonetheless, it is well to understand about avalanches, what causes them and when. It should even be noted that in the past skiers have been able to survive entrapment in very serious avalanches.

For simplicity, avalanches can be cataloged into two categories: wet and dry. Wet avalanches occur when warming temperatures—thaws or late-winter rains—break the adhesion between the ground and great chunks of piled-up snow. Suddenly and without warning these "unglued" masses can race down a slope, gaining speed up to 60 mph. If the avalanche is of any size at all, everything in its path is either crushed or buried or both.

Dry slides can be even worse, and their speeds have been calculated to far exceed 100 mph. These are triggered when storms or winds deposit more snow than a given mountain slope can hold in repose, or when the snow builds up into an un-

stable shape. When such a deposit breaks loose, the snow (often compressed to ice) can spread devastation at a speed impossible to describe. In Europe, where records have been kept for a long time, one Swiss avalanche of 1898 swept down a two-mile slope and partway up the opposite side of a valley, eliminating a whole town en route. Modern researchers into avalanches estimate that its velocity reached about 280 mph.

That was by no means the worst avalanche known. Others in Italy, Peru, and Austria have claimed more lives and wiped out more property. A 1955 avalanche raced past Blons, Austria, with such speed that it actually sucked people out of their houses. Besides the destructive force of the snow, people near dry avalanches have been suffocated by a dry "dust" of powdery snow that lingers behind over the scene.

North America has not experienced the horrible avalanches of Europe and elsewhere. One reason is better watershed conservation: Our mountain slopes have not been denuded by grazing and logged off for too many centuries, leaving them bare of protective cover. Another reason is that we now know more about avalanches, about how to detect avalanche conditions, how to prevent and avoid them. That includes even the smaller ones, which are the most likely to threaten skiers who wander too far from the commonly used trails.

Avalanches are unlikely to occur on slopes of less than 25 degrees. But beginning at about 35 degrees (a gradient similar to an average staircase) that critical zone begins where snow piled up deep should be avoided. Very rarely is it necessary to ski on such places for any reason. So why risk it?

Avalanches are far more likely to occur on certain kinds of slopes than others, even though the degree of steepness is the same. Unforested or bare (from clear-cutting timber) mountainsides are natural slide paths. So are any strips cleared by previous avalanches, which is a way of saying that these phenomena tend to recur in the same most "suitable" places. Heavily forested slopes or those punctuated with rough, uneven geologic formations seldom slide. But steep south-facing slopes must always be regarded with caution, especially in springtime after a late, heavy snowfall.

According to avalanche scientists, there are certain ideal situations where slides are most liable to be triggered. These are found just after a new snow of 10 inches or deeper quickly falls, when a sudden heavy snowfall exceeds an inch per hour, when strong winds have caused unnatural snow buildups, and when a warm wind blows steadily 12 mph or more. Beware of warm, fair weather just following a heavy storm, a condition as likely to stimulate skiers to action as it is to start snow sliding. Above-freezing temperatures (say, between 35 and 40 degrees) in spring cause deep thawing and wet avalanches. When those same temperatures are accompanied by rain, the avalanche potential becomes even more serious.

Any cross-country skier should know and be able to detect the obvious signs of avalanche danger, even though some of these may appear insignificant. The same overhanging cornices of snow and the deeply undercut snow cliffs that make spectacular photographs can suddenly break free and cause all snow accumulated below them also to start sliding. Stay away from overhangs, scenic as they may be.

It is well to be cautious when dry snow under the skis sifts like coarse sand into the ski wake instead of forming a sharp, slick track. Whenever damp snow in steep places falls away from under the skis and either rolls away downhill or breaks off in chunks, a skier is wise to hurry out of that area. Balls of otherwise undisturbed snow that break away and snowball downhill are telltale signs of poor, perhaps dangerous conditions. Avoid wind-packed or hard surface snow that covers soft snow on steep grades; this crust gives

away abruptly under pressure with a crunching sound but may be detectable only when ski poles break through as the skis pass over it smoothly. This kind of crust over soft snow can fracture off in large enough blocks to start a major slide below it.

Any ski tourer can totally avoid avalanches by steering clear of all hazardous and even questionable areas. Most blazed or popular ski trails skirt any dangers. It isn't cowardly in the least to detour any spot that is suspect.

If for some reason it *is* necessary to travel in avalanche country, maybe to help in a rescue, there are a number of rules to observe. Confine travel to early morning as much as possible because of increasing thaws (and danger) from midmorning onward until sundown. Select south slopes in preference to north slopes during cold weather, but exactly the opposite in springtime. Skiing across country is relatively safe during the early part of a storm, but tourers should find shelter somewhere as a heavy snow accumulates. It is wise to wait until a new fall has had a chance to become compacted before pushing on. It should be obvious that a skier should never cross any slope where cracks ominously open up ahead.

If some emergency leaves no alternative except to pass over a known dangerous avalanche situation, the following advice may be the difference between surviving and not. Cross a lower part of the slope or a part as low as possible. Try never to cross high up or around an outward-bulging (convex) part of any slope just under the summit. It is safest to proceed along the crests of ridges, staying back from the edges of sharp drop-offs.

In a party, members should cross any hazardous place one at a time. But they all can follow at intervals over any path that is negotiated safely by one member. Skiers should never go in bunches or roped together. If you are carrying a pack, straps should be loosened so that the pack can be discarded in an instant. In a really bad spot, remove your hands from ski pole loops, loosen ski or snowshoe bindings, and pull up the parka hood and secure it around the face, leaving only your eyes exposed.

No sensible skier should ever be caught in an avalanche. But it *has* happened by accident or mistake—and still has not always been fatal for skiers who knew how to react. Amazingly, many skiers have escaped from serious slides without even being greatly chilled, except mentally, perhaps.

If you are caught in a moving snowmass, which might move very slowly, maybe almost imperceptibly, at first, keep right on skiing fast to reach the nearest edge as quickly as possible and then continue well beyond it to stable ground. If that obviously isn't going to be possible, get rid of anything attached to your body—skis, pack, poles, the works—and start swimming. Swim vigorously to avoid being buried, on your back and with feet downhill if that is possible, but any old way to keep well on top of the slide. Try to drift toward an edge and out of the center. At the same time, try to keep your mouth and nose covered so as not to suffocate. When the avalanche stops, try to guarantee as much air space as possible around face and chest, because if the snow is wet, it may soon harden in that place.

A good percentage of avalanche victims have been rescued by the prompt action of others in the party. Every member should watch, try to mark, and distinctly remember where colleagues were last seen. As soon as the slide stops, make a quick search all along the slide line for survivors or for evidence of their location. Mark such spots with poles or other abandoned equipment. Then start digging and probing, wasting no time whatsoever. If there are no visible signs at which to begin a search, try the main snow pileup at the bottom or in any eddies where part of the slide has stopped. Do not give up easily or quickly, because avalanche victims have survived after long periods of entombment.

On finding an avalanche victim, first clear his nose and mouth of snow. If he isn't breathing, give mouth-to-mouth resuscitation. Look for fractures, treat for shock, and get the person away from the snow slide to as warm and secure a place as exists nearby. Pile on clothing, build a fire. Get help.

If it is necessary to ski a distance for help, only one should go while others stay with the rescued. The messenger skier should proceed at a moderate pace to avoid exhaustion and to be able to lead other rescuers back to the slide spot. Of course, he should be doubly careful to avoid getting lost himself and even running into another avalanche.

As stated earlier, the odds of encountering an avalanche are very low. But knowing about them should certainly help you to avoid them.

CHAPTER 13

WHERE TO SKI IN THE UNITED STATES

One of the most appealing aspects of ski touring is that it can be enjoyed in so many locales. Summer's now-snow-covered hiking trails, abandoned golf courses, power-line rights-of-way, or frozen streambeds all make fine trails. There are places specifically set up for ski touring, and they stretch almost without number across our northern tier of states and extend well into Canada and Alaska. We cannot here begin to list them all. I have attempted to note those that are outstanding in one way or another. I cannot quote prices, which, like the cost of everything else, rise almost steadily. It does remain true, however, that your ski-touring adventure will cost only a fraction of what a downhill excursion would.

A strong determining factor in cost is the distance you must travel to your destination. Obviously, driving thirty miles without the necessity of meals or an overnight en route will cost far less than jetting the family to a distant point. Ski-touring areas that were added to established downhill areas with lift tickets and chic restaurants will take a far larger bite of your budget than will skiing a state park. A midweek package saves money, and so does bringing your own trail lunch and snacks. Equipment rentals (usually about $6.00 per day) and lessons add somewhat to the cost, too.

THE NORTHEAST

In the northeastern sector of the country think first about the many state parks, especially if cost is a consideration. A letter of inquiry to any of the state capitals will produce a rash of bulletins and brochures full of information, far more than I can reproduce here.

But to list just a few of the feeless areas: In Connecticut take Exit 17 on Route 91 to Powder Ridge Ski Area in Middlefield. Guided tours, instruction, and equipment are available here; also, you can just ski on their five miles of trails and then continue on to the thirty or more miles of state hiking trails.

Beautiful, rugged Maine invites the free use of thirty-five miles of trails in Acadia National Park. Begin at the parking area off Route 198 in Northeast Harbor.

Five miles from Lake Placid in New York lies Mount Van Hoevenberg, again run by the state. Here are twelve miles of maintained trails laid out in loops. Areas vary in the degree of competence needed to enjoy them, and they're color coded. Closer to New York City is the popular Bear Mountain area, administered by the Palisades Interstate Park Commission. The drive north from George Washington Bridge is a scenic one but often there's no snow, so inquire first. Call 914-786-2701.

The state of New Hampshire offers skiing in White Mountain National Forest. A nice way to see it is to spend $1.00, which entitles you to ski the forest and adjacent private properties on a route that connects all inns, lodges, and hotels in the picturesque town of Jackson. Anything you'd care to purchase is available; buy nothing, if you wish. The address is Jackson Ski Touring Foundation, Jackson, NH 03846.

Also not far from New York City are Garnet Hill Lodges and Lake Minnewaska. Although they are not state parks or national forest areas, their nearness to New York City, if that's where you live, make them a good bet for an inexpensive trip. Garnet Hill is four hours from the city, northwest of Warrensburg on Thirteenth Lake in North River. Midweek packages are available, and there are several lodging alternatives from which to choose. Lake Minnewaska, in the Catskills, offers all the variety of accommodations, food, people, and *après*-ski life you'd expect. None of it is cheap, but think of the door-to-door limousine service from the metropolitan area.

Another inexpensive place is Bolton Valley in Vermont. Here there are twenty miles of trails that are part of the Long Trail System, and they're absolutely free. Experienced skiers would be most at home here.

Winter camping in a tent or snow cave is becoming more and more popular (see Chapter 6, devoted to that) and besides being good fun, it saves what are sometimes steep lodging prices. Many parks and private ski areas allow and even encourage camping, and a few have huts and cabins available for overnight use. Before deciding definitely on such an adventure, first call or write the area you intend to visit to be sure there are no strong objections.

If spending the night in a tiny alpine tent doesn't appeal to you, consider the opposite approach to winter ski-touring fun: Smuggler's Notch, in Jeffersonville, Vermont. This is a $10 million recreation community that can accommodate one thousand persons. Every option in instruction, equipment use, and guide services are available; or you may go it alone on twenty-five miles of trails, all of which are coded as to difficulty. Moonlight tours are also offered, and these are concluded with a wine and cheese feast.

To get here, drive to northern Vermont via Routes 89, 15, and, finally, 108; or take the bus to Burlington, where a complimentary bus from the Notch will pick you up.

Golf courses in many areas are simply deserted during the snowy months, and cruising up and over the terrain on your own, especially if it's nearby, is a pleasant experience. But many clubs have seen new opportunities for conducting business almost year 'round by offering golf during the warm months and ski touring during the cold. One of these is The Balsams Wilderness, a ninety-four-year-old summer resort on 15,000 acres in New Hampshire. They enthusiastically open their 450-bed hotel to ski tourers and offer lessons, marked and unmarked trails, lodging, and meals. Three others are in Massachusetts: The Wycoff Park Country Club in Holyoke is open during the winter, as Putterham Meadows Golf Course in Brookline, the closest ski-touring area for Bostonians. Waubeeka Touring Center in Williamstown has 150 rolling acres for the novice. Instruction is available, as is equipment to buy or rent. Proficient skiers may head toward adjacent Brodie Mountains or off to the east to Mount Greylock Reservation. There is a deluxe atmosphere at Greylock, with restaurants and motels of similar character.

Former Olympic skiers teach the novice at the Trapp Family Lodge (*The Sound of Music*) in Stowe, Vermont, for no more than you would pay elsewhere for a less expert instructor. A Learn-to-Ski package is offered, and it would be a good investment. The lodge rests on 1,000 acres of beautiful Vermont countryside and has 50 miles of trails, a cabin in the woods where lunch is served, and low rental prices.

If the group you would like to vacation with has varied outdoor interests, consider Green Trails Inn in Vermont. In addition to ski touring, this area promotes snowshoeing, sleigh riding, tobogganing, and sledding on more than 25 miles of marked trails. Green Trails Inn & Ski Touring Center is in Brookfield, south of Montpelier, off Route 89 near Randolph Center. You can reach it by Amtrak, which goes to Montpelier, or you can drive.

Another multiuse area to investigate is Evergreen Valley in East Stoneham, ME 04231. Of course, it's easy to find areas that cater to both alpine and Nordic skiing in the Northeast (Killington, Mount Snow, and Stratton, among others).

Ski touring at Jackson, New Hampshire, the hub of seventy miles of formal trails. Major ski areas that are part of the system are Tyrol, Black, and Wildcat mountains. NEW HAMPSHIRE OFFICE OF VACATION TRAVEL. PHOTO BY DICK SMITH.

Cross-country skiing at Bridgton, Maine. MAINE DEPARTMENT OF COMMERCE AND INDUSTRY. MDCI PHOTO.

Unplowed roads in New Hampshire's White Mountains provide endless ski touring. Mount Washington (6,288 feet) looms in the background. NEW HAMPSHIRE OFFICE OF VACATION TRAVEL. PHOTO BY JOHN P. WILSON.

Still in Vermont, the Woodstock Ski Touring Center, a half mile south of the 111-room Inn, has recently opened a 5-mile novice/intermediate trail, which brings the total mileage there to 40. The trail now connects the Touring Center with Kedron Valley Inn, and skiers can start at either end, availing themselves of refreshments, instruction, and lodging as desired—all in the town of Woodstock, of course.

New Jersey, Pennsylvania, and even Virginia have some ski-touring facilities, but as these areas are not in the snow belt, I strongly advise you to write or call before your arrival to be sure there is sufficient cover on the ground.

In New Jersey, Great Gorge Ski Area in McAfee might be your choice. This is mainly an alpine ski area complete with lift (and the lift fee), but once up you can ski ten miles of trails through the Hamburg Mountain Game Preserve. Great Gorge is easy to reach: Call 201-827-9146 for directions. There are several Morris County parks nearby that are free and that might offer ski touring on a casual basis. Write Morris County Parks and Recreation, County Office Building, Morristown, NJ 07960.

Sleepy Hollow Park in Sussex, New Jersey, has only a minimal snow cover. But after a heavy fall there are three hundred acres of gently sloping terrain to explore. For latest information call the area manager at 201-875-6211.

There are two state parks in Pennsylvania to consider: One is Black Forest, near Waterville—717-326-3576—and the other is French Creek State Park in Elverson—215-582-8125. Black Creek offers skiing only, so bring food and everything else you might need. French Creek has a relatively high elevation, and although it is in the southeastern part of the state, the chances of an adequate snow cover are better than average for Pennsylvania. Marked trails for beginners and more advanced skiers crisscross its six thousand acres.

Virginia has twenty miles of trails over the five thousand acres of Mount Rogers National Recreation Area. To check on the color of the ground, call Appalachian Outfitters in Blacksburg, 703-951-2600.

It would be impossible to describe or even mention every ski-touring area in the Northeast, but the state-by-state list below names some not covered above:

Connecticut

Blackberry River Inn, Norfolk

Maine

Akers Ski, 10 miles from Andover
Bear Mountain Village, Harrison
Pleasant Mountain, Pleasant Mountain
Saddleback, Rangeley
Sugarloaf, U.S.A., Kingfield
Sunday River, near Bethel

Massachusetts

Jug End Resort, South Egremont

New Hampshire

Bretton Woods, Bretton Woods
Emerson Hill, New Ipswich (near Fitchburg, Mass.)
Eastern Mountain Sports, Intervale
Gray Ledges, Grantham
Gunstock, Laconia
Loon Mountain, Lincoln
Pole and Pedal Shop trails, Henniket
Temple Mountain, four miles east of Peterborough
Waterville Valley, Waterville
Whitaker Woods, North Conway
Windblown, New Ipswich
Wolfeboro, Wolfeboro

New York

Adirondack Loj, Lake Placid
Apple Barn, Latham
Belleayre Mountain, Pine Hill
Country Hills Farm, Tully
Innsbruck, U.S.A., Binghamton
Lake Mohonk, New Paltz
Old Forge, Old Forge
Paleface Ski Center, Jay
Scotch Balley, Stamford
Williams Lake Hotel, Rosendale

Woodland ski travel on Sugarloaf Mountain, Maine. MAINE DEPARTMENT OF COMMERCE AND INDUSTRY. MDCI PHOTO.

Vermont

Burke Mountain, East Burke
Dakin's Vermont Mountain Shop, Ferrisburg
Darion Inn, East Burke
Edson Hill Manor, Stowe
Equinox Touring Center, Manchester
Farm Motor Inn and Country Club, Morrisville
Glen Ellyn, Waitsfield
Hermitage Inn, Wilmington
Highland Lodge, Greensboro
Killington, Killington
Mountain Top Inn, Chittenden
Okemo, Ludlow
Mount Snow, Mount Snow
Sonnenhof, Jay
Stratton Mountain, Stratton Mountain
Sugarbush Inn, Wareen
Viking Touring Center, Londonderry

For any special information about ski touring in the Green Mountain state write The Ski Touring Council, West Hill Road, Troy, VT 05868.

NORTH-CENTRAL STATES

Snowmobiles have caught the imagination of large parts of our north-central states. This is a sad thing for many ski tourers who cherish the quiet of the outdoors uninterrupted by the roar of snowmobiles. If peace is one of your requirements, investigate Blackhawk Ridge in Wisconsin. This area accommodates up to forty families on more than six hundred acres of private land and is closed to all snow machines. There are forty miles of trails, four of which are lighted for night touring, and you may camp here. Perhaps best of all, it is on the border of the Mazomanie Wildlife Area.

Two other spots, both in Michigan, are also safe from this latest user of the internal-combustion engine. The first, Birchwood Farm Lodge on Highway 131 in Harbor Springs, caters mainly to cross-country skiers, although there is plenty of downhill activity nearby. Lake Michigan can be glimpsed from some of the trails, and night tour-

ing with wine and fondue can be arranged. Birchwood accommodates 150 people on its 1,000 acres of land.

Ranch Rudolf is twelve miles southeast of Traverse City. The only machine allowed on the trails here is the one that grooms them. There are three trail loops for beginners and a thirteen-mile track for the expert on this landscape dotted with lakes, streams, and stands of trees. Two extra options are offered at Ranch Rudolf that you might like to explore. One is ski joring, with huskies instead of a horse pulling the skier, and the other is the availability of campsites where the ski tourer with backbone can overnight.

The overnighting ski tourer can also snow camp at Pine Mountain Ski Area in Iron Mountain, Michigan. Both Pine Mountain and Ranch Rudolf abut state forests, which, of course, add considerably to the land area available, and at no extra charge.

In Minnesota, Lutsen Resort in Lutsen is also the immediate neighbor to public land, the Superior National Forest. Lutsen has ten miles of maintained trails and in addition a huge network, which is available but is neither maintained nor patrolled.

One hundred fifty miles north of the Twin Cities is Quadna Mountain, which is a golf course during the warmer months and is open to ski touring during the winter. Be warned that snow machines are welcome here, but on the other hand this area also gives access to state forest land and with any luck you might escape to a peaceful area. Quadna Mountain is on the posh side, with cocktail lounges, a sauna, and other amenities.

If you are or plan to be in Minneapolis, ski Hennepin. Hennepin County Park has thirty miles of track for the free use of the public and is just twenty miles from the city. The purchase of a moderate-price annual ticket for the parking lot is necessary; for the itinerant skier, a small daily parking fee is collected. You have no gear? Rent it from Baker Hyland Lake Park Reserve nearby.

For the skier who feels that some sound instruction would improve his skills, Snowcrest in Somerset, Wisconsin, is the place. This is a noted school for the Professional Ski Instructors Association, and these instructors are available to teach the public, too. For no more than you would pay for lessons elsewhere, these teachers (certified in Norway) will give you the benefit of their expertise.

Just a hundred miles from the Twin Cities, in Rice Lake, Wisconsin, is Hardscrabble. The terrain is wooded and has ten miles of trails winding through the trees. Not too big. It's not unusual either in that rentals are available and there is a small trail fee. What is unusual is that nothing is for sale. Skiers are encouraged to bring their own lunches to cook (and the gear to do it with) and even their favorite bottle of wine. All lodging is five miles distant, and none is planned at the site. In fact, the owner has no plans for expansion at all. He likes the place the way it is and doesn't want a bar. That's unusual.

Some other places in the north-central area not mentioned above:

Michigan

Schuss Mountain, Mancelona
Shanty Creek Lodge, Bellaire
Sugar Loaf Village, Cedar

Minnesota

Sugar Hills Ski Area, Grand Rapids

Wisconsin

Green Lake, Green Lake
Snowcrest, Somerset
Telemark, Cable
Whitecap, Montreal

CALIFORNIA

California, which would, geographically, be considered part of the West, is taken as a separate unit, since the ski touring offered here springs from a different attitude from that which prevails elsewhere in the United States. The Golden State is home for the ultraserious skier who isn't out for a placid, relaxed tour, but is the core of the hard core. Here snow-survival tech-niques are taught, and ski treks into the mountains for days at a time are undertaken in a no-nonsense atmosphere. Certainly the more usual kind of skiing can be found in California, but it is not what prevails.

Consider High Sierra Wilderness Guide Service. They take groups of up to six skiers on trips of up to ten days' duration into the mountains at moderate rates. Write them c/o Alpenhaus Ski & Mountaineering Shop, 2760 Fulton Avenue, Sacramento, CA 95821.

Royal Gorge Ski Touring School in Soda Springs can set you up on a week-long trans-Sierra trip, too. All the usual kind of ski touring is also found here, and it includes a lodge for dormitory sleeping arrangements and a special tour to Donner summit.

Donner is the destination each spring of the Far West Ski Association, which escorts a group of skiers on the original route of the ill-fated 1846 Donner party. These trips are not ill-fated, however, and you can join the group leaving Tahoe-Donner Guest Ranch, P. O. Box 538, Truckee, CA 95734. No rentals, no trail fee.

A less strenuous journey is led on Saturdays and holidays by a ranger in the Inyo National Forest; being a public facility, it's free. Groups of five to twenty-five not only have a fine tour, but can also see free films and demonstrations on safety and attend wildlife and geology talks. Inyo is at Mammoth Lakes. Mammoth Lakes is also the home of Mammoth Cal-Nordic, which is typical of California's ski areas. They promote courses in mountaineering, cooking in the snow, winter survival, and information on avalanches. There are even classes for the blind and handicapped. You could well spend the night in a snow cave instead of Tamarack Lodge, where the less hardy stay.

The serious cross-country racer should consider Kirkwood Meadows Ski Touring Center in Kirkwood. Instruction for the novice is available, but the emphasis is on clinics for the expert who wants to compete in racing. They also have a snow survival course, which includes spending the night in a self-constructed snow cave.

Rock Creek Nordic in Bishop isn't the place for the less-than-confident skier, either. No shrinking violets should apply for the guided mountaineering tours or survival and safety clinics. Tours can be made to order, with a choice of many different destinations. Rock Creek adjoins the John Muir Wilderness area to which it has unlimited access, and if you're not out in a snowbank for the night you can be either at the lodge or in the wood-fire-heated cabin.

No discussion of ski possibilities in California would be complete without mention of Yosemite National Park and Squaw Valley.

Right on the edge of Lake Tahoe, Squaw Valley offers thirty-five to forty miles of marked and maintained trails free to the public. The usual instruction and rentals are offered plus the winter survival course that is inevitable in California. Tours of every kind are available, as are wine and cheese parties, ice skating, and even group sings. All in a magnificent if somewhat overpopulated setting. The address is Squaw Valley Nordic Ski Center, P. O. Box 2288, Olympic Valley, CA 95730.

Yosemite's Badger Pass may have been California's first organized ski area. Certainly with its magnificent scenery and usually idyllic weather it is a favorite winter sports area. The Nordic skier can move at his own pace over Yosemite's back country savoring the peace and beauty he finds. For the more adventurous there are overnight trips, which can be arranged through the Yosemite Mountaineering School at Curry Village. Instruction for both the beginner and the intermediate skier is available. A number of different lodging options are available, from housekeeping cottages to rooms at the gracious old Ahwahnee Hotel. Children receive special attention (and rates), and there is even a kennel for the dog. It's wise to have advance reservations from the Yosemite Park and Curry Company, Yosemite National Park, CA 95389.

Northern California's Lassen Park has snow until July, and its trails are free of charge for all. Childs Meadows is at the southern entrance and offers all you might need in the way of rental gear, instruction, and other services at reasonable cost. Both Lassen Park and Childs Meadows are in Mill Creek.

THE WEST

America's western states, traversed as they are by the Rocky Mountains, the Sierra-Nevadas, and a host of attendant ranges, provide some of the best skiing anywhere, together with great natural beauty and large amounts of air you may safely breathe while enjoying it.

Breckenridge in Colorado specializes in instruction, and skiers are divided into three categories of competence. There are five miles of level terrain, with some gentle slopes for the novice, twenty-five miles for the intermediate, and almost unlimited deep powder areas for the especially competent. Some mountaineering instruction is available, as are moonlight tours. Breckenridge, in addition to the ski touring, offers downhill slopes and various shops, restaurants, and lodging possibilities. They're at P. O. Box 705, Breckenridge, CO 80424.

Don't let the name frighten you off from Purgatory Ski Area, which also stresses the learning of technique. Instructors of unusual ability lead three tours, for the various levels of competence. Purgatory is in the San Juan Mountains; write P. O. Box 1311, Durango, CO 81301.

Several places in the West are geared to let you really see a broad swath of landscape. One is Crested Butte in the town of the same name, again in Colorado. The enthusiastic skier can cover twenty-five miles of marked trails over Pearl Pass and right down into Aspen, where he can begin all over again.

Arapaho National Forest has more miles of trails than you could cover in several years—480 of them, and all free. Just adjoining the forest is High Forest Inn (P. O. Box 119-X, Hideaway Park, CO 80450), which has rooms and less expensive dormitory accommodations. If you tire of the national forest, take a tour of the old town of Leadville or a whole-day trip to Dinosaur National Monument.

The competent skier who wants to see and experience the Rocky Mountains in the winter might start from Lake Eldora and see some of the more lofty peaks, a few of which are cloud-capped. If you are venturing out on your own (guided tours are available), do get a U. S.

The Wallowa Mountains in northeastern Oregon are the background for this skiing scene in the Lick Creek area southeast of Joseph in Wallowa County. OREGON STATE HIGHWAY PHOTO.

Geodetic Survey map in Boulder first. The trails are not patrolled, and the weather is noted for its rapid ups and downs. Indigenous wildlife is often encountered, and this could be a memorable time. Lake Eldora is in Nederland, CO 80466.

For another wilderness experience consider Glacier National Park in Montana. The high-country skiing is excellent for the experienced, skilled person. This is usually tackled on a group basis, and previous consultation with the park ranger is mandatory. No food or rentals are available, and so the would-be winter visitor must think ahead, bring his own, and be more than usually self-sufficient. Lake McDonald sits on lower ground and is the preference of less vigorous individuals. Glacier National Park Headquarters, West Glacier, MT 59936, is the correct place for inquiries.

Exhilarating adventure can also be found at Hoodoo Ski Bowl in Camp Sherman, OR 97730. The emphasis here is on alpine touring, which is done on equipment heavier than the usual Nordic skis. Hoodoo borders on the Pacific Crest Trail, and most skiing is done on Forest Service land between Mount Washington and Mount Jefferson. Consequently there is no charge. At this writing the only lessons given are through the University of Oregon. There is no lodging at Hoodoo, the closest being at Black Butte Ranch ten miles away.

Several western states other than California have areas that offer the California-type experience. Rocky Mountain Expeditions, P. O. Box 576, Buena Vista, CO 81211, will take an experienced, hardy skier on a rugged trip for from one to five days on a real winter mountain expedition. The trip is a back-country one into the Continental Divide area. The destination could be Mount Elbert, Colorado's highest peak. Arctic expedition tents or cabins shelter the adventurer through the night. Trips are tailored to individual needs and include guides, shelter, food, and most equipment.

Even intermediate skiers can join in for a one-to-three-day backpack trip with guide at Cascade Corrals in Washington. Arrangements are flexible and include the possibility of having a helicopter fly skier and gear to a remote area. The skier then spends the day touring the new area, ending, by evening, at the highway, where he's picked up. The alternatives are numerous, and the costs depend on individual arrangements. Cascade is at

Stehekin, WA 98852. The Northwest Alpine Guide Service out of Seattle will take groups of limited numbers on weekends along the deepest glacier-carved canyon in the state, Icicle Creek. Shelter for the participants is in tents with insulated floors. The more usual day lessons, group trips, and classes in technique and waxing are given, too. Obtain particulars from the Service at P. O. Box 80345, Seattle, WA 98108.

No discussion of the West is complete without mention of the most famous downhill areas. The three that everyone knows best in Colorado are Steamboat, Vail, and Snowmass. All three places have enlarged their scope to include the cross-country advocate. It's Scandinavian Lodge at Steamboat Village for the Nordic skier. In addition to the usual, there are shops, a sauna, and a gym, plus clinics on everything from how to get into the ski lodge business yourself to the care and selection of equipment. The rental gear is of top quality, and there is no trail fee.

Vail, too, welcomes the Nordic tourist. Instruction is given on a golf course, and there are 145 miles of unmarked trails extending from there in all directions. Because much of it is challenging, it is recommended that you go with a guide. Looking like coal miners, tourers can don lighted helmets and take a guided nighttime swing around the area led by a guide. A hot snack is provided en route. Vail, like Steamboat, is self-contained and has everything. Write the Ski Touring School, P. O. Box G, Avon, CO 81620.

Snowmass Ski Touring Center in Aspen, CO 81611 is the third of the big three, and several sorts of lodging are available right on the mountain. Lessons are given at the going rate, and equipment rents for less than at other places. The touring school here too is situated on what, in the summer, is a golf course.

Sun Valley, ID 83353 has everything from condominiums to bowling lanes and more ways to ski than you could think of in a year. There is a day-long bus trip with stops en route for skiing particularly scenic areas. How about an after-dark excursion on skis to a touring cabin where an abundant, delicious meal awaits? Helicopter trips into the back country are popular, allowing quiet wilderness skiing. Or fly one way and ski the other. Public skiing is allowed on a hundred miles of marked and maintained trails, and every sort of lesson/lodging package is available.

For the enthusiastic skier who wants a new ex-

Cross-country skiing in deep snow on Mount Hood, Oregon. OREGON STATE HIGHWAY PHOTO.

Ski tourers gliding past a herd of elk in Yellowstone National Park, Wyoming. WYOMING TRAVEL COMMISSION PHOTO.

perience just the opposite of those mentioned, Craters of the Moon is the place. A strange terrain of snow-covered solidified lava flows in weird shapes offers a unique ski tour adventure. Designated campgrounds with fireplaces are here, but nothing else. Nothing. Wood for a fire must be brought in; there is no electricity and no supplies available at all. However, these can be purchased in the town of Arco, eighteen miles distant. All arrangements should be made through the Superintendent, Craters of the Moon National Monument, P. O. Box 29, Arco, ID 83213.

Big Sky is another huge new development. It is in the Spanish Peaks Primitive Area of Montana. Beautiful scenery is typical of the area, and thirty-five miles of trails wander through it. Rental costs are exceptionally high, but there is no trail fee. Lodging is varied, abundant, and high-priced. Big Sky is in western Montana and has its own Zip Code: 59716.

Jackson Hole, Wyoming, has long been known for its downhill skiing in the town of Jackson and also at nearby Teton Village. Less known is the cross-country skiing here and in adjoining Targhee National Forest and Grand Teton National Park. Grand Targhee Resort in Alta, Wyoming, is north of Jackson Hole and south of Yellowstone National Park. It caters mainly to downhill skiers, but has instruction and gear rental for ski tourers and miles of marked trails, only seven miles of which are maintained. This area is reached from the west, through Driggs, Idaho.

The official downhill opening date in Jackson is usually about the ninth of December, but cross-country enthusiasts can begin just as soon as there's a sufficient cover, often weeks earlier. Snow remains in the higher elevations into June

with a few muddy patches; count on widespread really usable cover until April.

Several shops in town have touring gear for rent and guides available to take the visitor to some of the most beautiful areas in the United States. Snow King Mountain is for alpine skiing, but it will also take the tourer away from the throng on the slopes into the wilderness nearby.

Jackson Hole Ski & Sports Shop on the village square is also the home of Sundance Tours and Rentals. Moderately priced skis, boots, poles, gaiters, and waxes are available, as are tours for a single skier, or a group of up to six. Technique sessions are given on an oval track in Grand Teton National Park, and special arrangements

This magnificent sight is Grotto Geyser at Yellowstone National Park, Wyoming. ERWIN A. BAUER.

The end of the trail for a ski
traveler in Sun Valley, Idaho. SUN
VALLEY NEWS BUREAU PHOTO.

A party skiing cross-country under
the leadership of Nordic champion
Leif Odmark in Sun Valley.
SUN VALLEY NEWS BUREAU PHOTO.

for overnights or extended tours into magnificent back country can be made. Knowledgeable, experienced guides are the rule. Sundance also has an office at Teton Village.

Ski touring in Grand Teton National Park has zoomed in popularity in the past few years with the general growth in this type of outdoor activity. The novice can betake himself to the flat-country trails that are the early parts of the trails leading to Taggart and Bradley lakes. The more confident skier can continue on to the challenging terrain closer to the lakes. Trails are marked but not maintained; generally they are used enough so that breaking new trail isn't necessary. A particularly nice tour begins at the Whitegrass Ranger Station, climbs to seventy-two hundred feet to overlook Phelps Lake, and then continues on into Death Canyon. No winter facilities are maintained at this park, and all supplies must be brought in; the nearest town is, of course, Jackson. For information and maps write Grand Teton Park Headquarters, P. O. Box 67, Moose, WY 83012.

Yellowstone National Park caters more and more to winter tourists. This area of northwestern Wyoming is a fairyland, with green, yellow, and blue thermal pools bubbling in the deep snows. The elk, buffalo, and deer are concerned more with survival than with the eyes of a passing skier. For three months, from before Christmas until mid-March, Snow Lodge at Old Faithful (which remains faithful even during the winter) is open. A good six-day Ski-Tourer package beginning either in Jackson or in Bozeman, Montana, has been established, and for the adventurous, experienced skier, the Nordic Package: a five-day, four-night tour with a dependable guide into a beautiful, remote area of the park. All new prices and information are available from the Yellowstone Park Company, Yellowstone National Park, WY 82190.

Do be warned that snowmobiles are welcomed, too. According to the rules they must stay on the roads, but bad behavior and tracks on the snow too often betray a callous disregard of the regulations. By all means inquire as to the dates of snowmobile races and plan to come to Yellowstone at another time. Many visitors feel that the inclusion of snowmobiles in the park's program detracts from the atmosphere that was intended to prevail in our national parks.

Timberline Lodge is the starting point for a cross-country skiing party on Mount Hood. OREGON STATE HIGHWAY PHOTO.

Snow machines are permitted in parts of Grand Teton Park, too, but they are easier to escape here than is possible in Yellowstone.

Additional ski-touring areas in the West:

Colorado

Ashcroft, Aspen
C & G Touring, Fraser
Chuck Fothergill's, Aspen
Copper Mountain Touring, Frisco
Keystone, Dillon

Montana

The Big Mountain, Whitefish
Bridger Bowl, Bozeman
Montana Snow Bowl, Missoula

Oregon

Mount Bachelor, Bend
Mount Hood (several areas)

Washington

Mission Ridge, Wenatchee
49° North, Chewelah

THE SOUTHWEST

Angel Fire at Eagle Nest, NM 87718 was recently purchased by a large corporation, which has since put $5.5 million into developing the area. There are accommodations of all sorts and many miles of trail for the ski tourer, some marked and maintained, plus large areas of land for the skier who sets his own track.

Another large area, perhaps better known, is Park City, just thirty-five miles from Salt Lake City, Utah. Park City caters to the downhill skier, but it now also has fifty miles of track for the alpine enthusiast. Besides the shops, restaurants, and bars, the visitor can tour the century-old mining town right next door. Instructors and supplies for winter mountain camping trips can be arranged at Wolfe's Ski Shop, Park City Touring Center, P. O. Box 27, Park City, UT 84060.

Happily, the state of Utah is spangled with national parks and monuments for the use of all. Bryce Canyon National Park, with its spectacular spires and canyons of eroded red sandstone, has steep trails and hairpin curves to negotiate and is terrain for the experienced cross-country skier. Beginners keep to the rim drive. There are no facilities of any sort here. Write to the Superintendent, Bryce Canyon National Park, Bryce Canyon, UT 84717.

Cedar Breaks, in southwestern Utah, has good trails with fine views. The road that connects it to Dixie National Forest is skiable too and leads to the forest's own network of casual tracks. The Superintendent, Cedar Breaks National Monument, 491 South Main, Cedar City, UT 84720 will inform you that the closest lodging is twenty miles distant at Brianhead Ski Resort and will give any other information you need.

There are no facilities at Zion Park, but the Lava Point area is open for the confident cross-country skier. The road is open but not plowed, and often only four-wheel-drive vehicles can negotiate it. The closest lodging is at Hurricane or Springdale, a short distance from the entrance. Write to the Superintendent, Zion National Park, Springdale, UT 84767.

Bandelier National Monument in New Mexico has the fantastic scenery of so much of our Southwest, but the tracks here are difficult in the precipitous canyons and there are no winter facilities for skiers. Write to the Superintendent, Bandelier National Monument, Los Alamos, NM 87544.

Individually arranged trips for up to six skiers can be arranged with Trail Adventures De Chama, 5839 Idlewilde Lane, S.E., Albuquerque, NM 87108. They'll take the group with two qualified guides for up to a week of winter camping in the mountains.

Possibly the least developed ski area in the Southwest is Snowland Ski Area. No rentals or instruction here; there are no shops, and the nearest lodging is eight miles distant in Fairview. But the tourer who cherishes peace and solitude has thirty-two miles of trail to enjoy. Snowland is in the center of Utah in the Manti-LaSal National Forest. Write to Snowland, Fairview Canyon, Fairview, UT 84629.

Other ski areas in the Southwest:

New Mexico

Taos Ski Valley, Taos Ski Valley

Nevada

Slide Mountain, Mount Rose, Reno

Utah

Brighton Ski Bowl, Brighton
Powder Mountain, Eden
Snow Basin, Ogden
Snowbird, Snowbird
Park West, Park City

There is also ski touring in and around the major ski areas around Flagstaff, Arizona.

CHAPTER 14

WHERE TO SKI IN CANADA AND ALASKA

THE MARITIME PROVINCES

Canada's maritime provinces of New Brunswick, Nova Scotia, and Newfoundland have some cross-country skiing, and of the three, New Brunswick has the largest number. There are eleven spots in this province. Some of them are open only in the afternoon, with skiing continuing on into the night. On weekends and over holidays however, they swing into high gear and are in operation mornings, too.

Sugarloaf Provincial Park is in the snow belt of northern New Brunswick and is the preferred ski area at Campbellton Mount Kodiak. Snow conditions are said to be consistently good and the trails well groomed. Accommodations are available in the nearby town.

Other good places are Mount Douglas, forty-five miles north of Saint John, Mount Farlange at Edmundston, and Crabbe Mountain, which lies forty miles from Fredericton.

Crossing over the isthmus of Chignecto, the skier arrives at Nova Scotia, a peninsula approximately 375 miles long by 50 to 100 miles wide. The town of Truro lies at the head of the south-erly finger of the Bay of Fundy, and forty-five miles to the northwest is Wentworth Hostel, run by the Canadian Youth Hostels Association from its headquarters at Halifax. The cost of lessons and gear rental is exceedingly low, and the unmaintained thirty-five miles of cross-country trails are free for skiers' use. The Hostels Association does, however, gratefully accept donations toward the purchase of trail-setting equipment.

Newfoundland is known for its friendliness, and so the visiting skier has no trouble finding his way from Corner Brook on the west side of the island to Marble Mountain, just eight miles away. The ski tourer has a wide choice of tracks here, from very easy to steep and tricky. There is another ski area in Newfoundland and it is remote, accessible only by Eastern Provincial Airlines or Quebecair from Montreal. Smokey Mountain is at Labrador City and has a complete range of services and accommodations at the base. In addition, Smokey Mountain claims skiable snow into June.

In Quebec several resorts cater almost exclusively to the trail skier. Miles of old and new trails are maintained. CANADIAN GOVERNMENT TRAVEL BUREAU PHOTO.

A class for cross-country skiers at The Parkers' Lodge, Val-David, in the Laurentian country north of Montreal. CANADIAN GOVERNMENT OFFICE OF TOURISM PHOTO.

QUEBEC

This eastern province is so large that it is usually divided into areas: two in the east and two in the west, for purposes of clarity. Eastern Quebec is composed, so far as the skier is concerned, of the eastern townships and Quebec City.

Within a reasonable radius of Quebec City there are three ski areas: Mont-Ste.-Anne, Lac Beauport, and Stoneham. All are easy to reach by buses, which connect them with each other and with downtown Quebec. Mont-Ste.-Anne is twenty-seven miles east of the city and is the most distant. The season here, since the new development of the north side of the peak, extends into late spring, and the terrain area has almost doubled. Lodges for day use are at both base and summit. In a sheltered valley fifteen miles north of the city lies Lac Beauport, the traditional vacation area. There are lodges here too, and French cuisine to coax the skier inside sooner than he'd planned. Stoneham offers ten good trails and a large day lodge. It is nineteen miles from Quebec.

The longest seasons in eastern Canada are found here in the eastern townships of the province of Quebec. Situated in a natural snow belt area, they lie just north of the U.S. border and are composed of six major areas southeast of Montreal. They are Owl's Head, Glen Mountain, Mont Sutton, Bromont, Mont Ordord, and Mont Echo, all easily reached from the Eastern Township's autoroute. A single ticket permits the skier to use any of the areas.

There are no fewer than six major ski areas within a radius of twelve to sixty miles of Ottawa. One, Calabogie Peaks, happens to be across the border in Ontario, but it is near the capital, and the pleasures of this city's life are undisputed. The other five are Camp Fortune, Vorlage, Edelweiss Valley, Mont Cascade, and Mont Ste.-Marie. Reach all of them via Highway 11.

The heaviest concentration of skiing hills for any area of equal size in the world is in the Laurentian Mountains, less than an hour's drive north of Montreal. This forty-square-mile area is the most highly developed year-'round resort area in Canada. It can all be reached via the Laurentian autoroute. St.-Sauveur-des-Monts, forty miles from Montreal, is the first the skier reaches. After that there's Piedmont, Mont-Gabriel, St.-Adèle, Ste.-Marguerite, Val-Tremblant, Chateau Montebello, and Far Hills. The final spot is Mont Tremblant. All offer quality skiing.

In addition, the provincial government provides miles of track at Duchesnay Forestry Station and three parks: Laurentides, Mont-Ste.-Anne, and Mont Oreford. For more information on these public areas, write to the Director General of Tourism for Quebec, Canada, 17 West 50th Street, New York, NY 10020.

ONTARIO

Of all the Canadian provinces, Ontario shares the longest border with the United States, stretching in an irregular line north of the Great Lakes from Minnesota on the west to New York on the east. The cross-country ski areas, however, are concentrated mainly in three areas of the province: the Toronto area; the Georgian Bay area, which is the eastern lobe of Lake Huron; and the Thunder Bay area near Isle Royale on the northwestern shore of Lake Superior.

The Toronto area is most accessible from the States, and ninety miles northeast in Kimberley is the Talisman Resort Hotel. It has a good range of trails for both the beginner and the more advanced skier and all facilities for the visitor. Georgian Peaks is generally jammed with Toronto skiers on weekends but is a good bet for fine skiing during the week. Georgian Peaks has the highest vertical drop in Ontario and some of the best runs.

Formosa Springs Brewery in Barrie runs Octoberfest, a recreational area on seventy acres of land just forty-eight miles north of Toronto. The use of the cross-country trails, the ice-skating rink (which is lighted at night), and the snowshoe nature trails is free. There are two hundred sets of ski-touring equipment and fifty pairs of snowshoes offered for use free of charge, too. Do bring your own ice skates. The Barrel House is a forty-eight-hundred-square-foot lounge available for special occasions, and the Keg Inn has hot snacks at moderate cost.

Blue Mountain Park in Collingwood near Georgian Bay has both instruction and equipment available at costs that are high for Canada—about what you'd pay in the United States. It offers good touring trails on open land, and a favorite is Bruce Trail, which rides on a high ridge overlooking the bay.

Horseshoe Valley is a golf course during the summer and has eleven miles of groomed trails for the skier during the winter. Most trails are short, but the atmosphere is congenial. Horseshoe Valley Resort is in Barrie.

Limberlost and Hidden Valley are both in Huntsville, some miles to the east of Georgian Bay. Limberlost Lodge is a large, fairly expensive spot that includes over 135 kilometers of marked and maintained trails. Weekend trips to a cabin and midweek packages are popular, as are sleigh rides, ice skating, and saunas. Stay at the lodge or rustic cabins with fireplaces in the back country right at the border of Algonquin Park.

Hidden Valley Ski Club charges no trail fee, and its gentle terrain in the Muskoka resort area appeals to the novice skier, although the intermediate class would find some interest here, too.

The Loch Lomond area on Loch Lomond Highway in Thunder Bay has tracks down each side of a valley whose vertical height is eight hundred feet. There are two trails on the north face complex: Jolly Giant and Giant Slalom. Both offer fine skiing.

Mount Norway on Highway 61, which runs along the shore of Lake Superior, is a small area with some of the best skiing around, including

Cross-country skiers in Horseshoe Valley, west of Orillia, Ontario. ONTARIO MINISTRY OF INDUSTRY AND TOURISM.

Thunder Bowl run. There are three major tracks and seven subsidiary trails.

Recently opened is the largest ski development in Thunder country, the Big Chief area at Mount McKay. Before the new areas were opened McKay was regarded as the top intermediate-class area, and now the new trails add much more challenge for those willing and able to accept them. Mount McKay is just three miles south of the international airport.

Trail skiing at Limberlost Lodge, near Huntsville, Ontario. CANADIAN GOVERNMENT TRAVEL BUREAU PHOTO.

Ski touring at an elevation of 7,200 feet in Banff National Park in the Rocky Mountains of Alberta. CANADIAN GOVERNMENT OFFICE OF TOURISM PHOTO.

THE PRAIRIE PROVINCES

Canada's central prairie provinces are generally flat land drained by many rivers with a heavy sprinkling of swamps, ponds, and lakes. They are the least suited to ski touring of any section in Canada. However, 107 miles southwest of Winnipeg is Holiday Mountain at La Rivière, with tows that operate all day every day from December to April. Skiing is also good at Mount Agassiz in Riding Mountain National Park near McCreary and Mount Glenorkley near Brandon. Both have overnight accommodations for the visiting skier. Don't overlook Falcon Lake in Manitoba's Whiteshell Provincial Park, 96 miles east of Winnipeg, which offers all winter sports. Write the Director of Manitoba Tourism, Winnipeg, Manitoba R3B 2E7, Canada, for present conditions.

ALBERTA

Banff and Jasper national parks in this province are justly famous throughout the world for their magnificent scenery. Lake Louise, equally well known, is part of Banff, and instruction and rentals are available here. Visitors may stay at the Skoki Lodge, which is opened for several months each winter for this purpose. There are extensive facilities of all kinds here, and the skier may also use more than sixty miles of trails in Banff Park free of charge. The trails are marked and maintained by the rangers.

Sunshine Lodge, also at Banff, has its own trails and access to the park's trails too. The skiing here is on fine snow in bowls. An early-spring tour toward Mount Assiniboine is popular.

Three miles from Banff is Mount Norquay, the destination of advanced skiers. The intermediate class goes here too, but generally stays with Wishbone Trail, which is only of moderate difficulty.

Jasper Park has 800 miles of trails of its own, and 11 miles from here is the Marmot Basin Ski School, with high-bowl skiing and long, swinging tracks from the 8,557-foot peak. The two networks are contiguous for a large choice of terrain for the ski tourer.

BRITISH COLUMBIA

Canada's westernmost province of British Columbia has a tremendous annual snowfall on its nearly endless Rocky Mountain ranges. Skiing is popular, and there are many places devoted to it.

Not far from Penticton on Route 97, which extends down into the state of Washington, is Apex-Alpine in the Okanagan Valley. This entire area is known for its dry, fluffy, fast snow, and the trails are for the experienced skier. They are steep and twisting. This area, which also has trails for the intermediate skier, is twenty-two miles from Penticton on Green Mountain Road.

Big White shares the Okanagan Valley with Apex but concentrates more on skiing for the skier of average accomplishments. The tracks are long and gradual from open, flatter summits. Big White's home base is Kelowna.

The area immediately surrounding Vancouver has a number of ski areas. The least expensive is Burke Mountain, with thirty-five to forty miles of trail. Cross Country City has lodging at nearby Prince George and inexpensive rentals and lessons too, on trails of equal length to those of Burke Mountain.

At the end of a five-minute ride on the Grouse Mountain Skyride from the North Vancouver terminal you are at the top third of Grouse Mountain, where you can ski night or day. Lodging is at the Grouse Nest.

Seventy-five miles north of Vancouver in Garibaldi Provincial Park lies Whistler Mountain, with a tremendous vertical drop of 4,280 feet and deep powder bowls at the top, with runs to an evergreen base. For solitary skiing, accomplished ski tourers can take a helicopter to nearby glacier areas and make the first marks in powder snow.

Other ski areas in British Columbia are within a reasonable distance of the U.S. border; in fact, some are quite close.

A two-hour drive from Spokane is Red Mountain, which specializes in trails for the expert. This is a two-mountain complex: Red Mountain and Granite Mountain. You may overnight at the Red Shutter Inn in Rossland.

North of our Glacier National Park in Montana is the Kimberley ski area for the skier of modest skill. It's fifty miles north of the border. There are seventeen miles of groomed trails here,

In Garibaldi Provincial Park, British Columbia, the snowfalls are so heavy that skiing is possible well into June. CANADIAN GOVERNMENT TRAVEL BUREAU PHOTO.

and accommodations of several types are available at Kimberley.

In Manning Provincial Park on the Washington border and 145 miles east of Vancouver is Gibson Pass. This is a lively area to which families gravitate. Rentals are available here as well as instruction and two hundred miles of trail.

Perhaps the most distant area from the U.S. border is Silver Star, which is fourteen miles from Vernon, north of Penticton on Route 97. Silver Star is a family area too, with rentals and lessons plus an enjoyable Winter Carnival in February each year.

ALASKA

For the cross-country journey of a lifetime, you can explore Mount McKinley Park on the north face of the Alaska Range during winter. The huge snow pack, which is the most usual condition for this magnificent area, affords some of the most adventurous skiing anywhere. Denali Dog Tours and Wilderness Freighters uses dog teams to pull sleds that accompany the ski tourer or ski mountaineer. This way, not burdened with equipment, the skier sees more with more ease faster than would be possible under backpacks. Nights are spent in old patrol cabins or heated tent camps. All information and bookings are from Eberhard's Sport Shop, 307 East Northern Lights & Denali, Anchorage, AK 99755.

Genet Expeditions in Talkeetna, AK 99676 also takes groups of four or five for extended journeys into the McKinley country. With luck you may see bear, moose, Dall sheep, and caribou, and you can enjoy some climbing and glacier training there, too. Skiers fly one way or round trip with a bush pilot to either Ruth Glacier Amphitheatre or Pirate Lake—an unforgettable experience for the hardy, practiced skier.

More accessible areas in Alaska have skiing, too. Alyeska, in Girwood, near Anchorage, has both downhill and Nordic skiing, and Nordic Ski Clubs maintain trails in Chugach State Park. The club is in Fairbanks, and for particulars write P. O. Box 5-111, College, AK 99701.

A good way to reach Alaska is to fly Western Airlines to Anchorage and depart from there.

APPENDIXES

REFERENCES ON SKIING, SNOWSHOEING, AND ALLIED SUBJECTS

Backpacker magazine (bimonthly: February, April, June, August, October, and December), 65 Adams Street, Bedford Hills, N.Y. 10507.

Backpacking Equipment (a consumer guide), 65 Adams Street, Bedford Hills, N.Y. 10507.

Bauer, Erwin A. *Hunting with a Camera*. New York: Winchester Press, 1974.

————. *Outdoor Photography*. New York: E. P. Dutton, 1965. Second edition, revised and updated, 1974. Book Division, Times Mirror Magazine, Inc.

Brady, M. Michael. *Ski Cross-Country*. New York: The Dial Press, 1974.

Caldwell, John. *The New Cross-Country Ski Book*. Brattleboro, Vt.: The Stephen Green Press, fourth edition, 1973.

Kinmont, Vikki, and Axcell, Claudia. *Simple Foods for the Pack*. San Francisco: Sierra Club, 1976.

Kjellstrom, Bjorn. *Be Expert with Map and Compass*. New York: Charles Scribner's Sons, 1976.

Lederer, William J., and Wilson, Joe Pete. *Complete Cross-Country Skiing and Ski Touring*. New York: W. W. Norton & Company, 1970.

Manning, Harvey. *Backpacking One Step at a Time*. Seattle, Wash., Recreational Equipment Inc., 1972.

Maye, Patricia. *Field Book of Nature Photography*. San Francisco: Sierra Club, 1974.

Miller, Mike, and Wayburn, Peggy. *Alaska, the Great Land*. San Francisco: Sierra Club, 1974.

Osgood, William, and Hurley, Leslie. *The Snowshoe Book*. Brattleboro, Vt.: The Stephen Greene Press. Third printing, January 1973.

Prater, Gene. *Snowshoeing*. Missoula, Mont.: Mountaineers, 1975.

Riviere, Bill. *Back Country Camping*. Garden City, N.Y.: Doubleday & Company, 1971. Dolphin Books Edition, 1972.

Ski magazine (monthly), 380 Madison Avenue, New York, N.Y. 10017.

Tokle, Art, and Luray, Martin. *Complete Guide to Cross-Country Skiing and Touring*. New York: Vintage Books, Random House, 1974.

Van Lear, Denise. *The Best About Backpacking*. San Francisco: Sierra Club, 1974.

Wiik, Sven, and Summer, David. *Regnery Guide to Ski Touring*. Chicago: Henry Regnery Company, 1974.

WHERE TO WRITE

For literature on state parks and privately owned touring areas in states where organized ski touring is offered, write to the following:

Alaska: Alaska Travel Division, Pouch E, Juneau, AK 99801.

Colorado: Holubar Mountain Ltd., P. O. Box 7, Boulder, CO 80302. Also U. S. Forest Service, Building 85, Denver Federal Center, Denver, CO 80225.

California: Far West Ski Association, 812 Howard Street, San Francisco, CA 94103. The FWSA publishes *Ski Touring Annual* every year, listing events, clubs, and where you can find instruction, lodging, and huts.

Maine: State of Maine Publicity Bureau, 929 Gateway Circle, Portland, ME 04102.

Michigan: Southeast Michigan Travel and Tourism Association, Executive Plaza, 1200 6th, M-150, Detroit, MI 58226.

Montana: Advertising Unit, Room 53, Montana Highway Department, Helena, MT 59601. Also U. S. Forest Service (Northern Region), Federal Building, Missoula, MT 59801.

New Hampshire: Division of Economic Development, P. O. Box 856, Concord, NH 03301.

New York: State Department of Environmental Conservation, Albany, NY 12202, or State Office of Parks and Recreation, Albany, NY 12223. Also write the Ski Touring Council, 51-01 39th Avenue, Long Island City, NY 11104 for their *Ski Touring Guide* ($2.25).

Ontario: Ministry of Industry and Tourism, Travel Service Branch, Hearst Block, 900 Bay Street, Toronto, Ontario M7A 1S6, Canada. Ask for the booklet *Ontario Winter Adventures.*

Oregon/Washington: Northwest Alpine Guide Service, Inc., P. O. Box 80345, Seattle, WA 98108. Also U. S. Forest Service, Region 6, P. O. Box 3623, Portland, OR 97208.

Wisconsin: Write the Wisconsin Department of Natural Resources, Bureau of Commercial Recreation, P. O. Box 450, Madison, WI 53701 for the brochure/location guide, *Wisconsin Ski Touring Opportunities.*

General Information: The Ski Touring Council, West Hill Road, Troy, VT 05868 publishes *Ski-Touring Guide* ($2.00) and an annual *Schedule* ($2.50) outlining ski-touring activity in New York, New Jersey, Pennsylvania, and New England. The Appalachian Mountain Club, 5 Joy Street Boston, MA 02108, also has information on touring in Massachusetts, Rhode Island, Maine, and New Hampshire.

LOCAL AREA TRAIL GUIDES

Ski Touring Guide to New England, ed. Medora Bass, 2nd ed. (Eastern Mountain Sports, Boston, MA 02215, 1973), 286 pages in a 3-ring binder ($4.50), lists trails and areas in Connecticut, Massachusetts, Vermont, New Hampshire, and Maine.

Ski Touring Guide, Ski Touring Council, Troy, VT 05868, 92-page booklet (1973–74) ($2.00), primarily gives trails and areas in Vermont and New York State, with a few in other East Coast states.

Ski Tours in California, David Beck (Far West Ski Association) (c/o Federation of Western Outdoor Clubs, 4534½ University Way, NE, Seattle, WA 98115, 1972) ($4.95), gives some advice on touring plus descriptions of 38 tours in the Sierras and some ski mountaineering routes.

Ski Minnesota, A Cross-Country Skier's Guide to Minnesota and Western Wisconsin, Gary Noren and Dwight Olsen (published by the authors in co-operation with the North Star Ski Club, 1973), 95-page 8½-by-11-inch, spiralbound, stenciled ($2.75). Lists 77 areas with maps for most.

A Guide to Ski Touring Covering Colorado, Southern Wyoming, and New Mexico, ed. Morgan Queal (Rocky Mountain Division,

United States Ski Association, 1972), 54-page booklet ($2.00), lists trails in major ski areas and national parks along with quadrangle map information.

Washington Nordic Tours, Brad Bradley (Signpost, 16812 36th Avenue West, Lynnwood, WA 98036) ($3.95).

Aspen Tourskiing & Cross-Country, Raymond N. Auger (Columbine Books, P. O. Box 2841, Aspen, CO 81611), 59-page booklet (1971) ($1.75).

Adventure Trip Guide, 1,000 selected vacation ideas (Adventure Guides, Inc., 3 East 57th Street, New York, NY 10022).

Oregon Ski Tours, Doug Newman and Sally Sharrad, a guide to 65 cross-country trails (Backpacker, Bellows Falls, VT 05101) ($4.95).

REGIONAL OFFICES OF THE U. S. FOREST SERVICE

Following are the addresses of the nine regional offices of the U. S. Forest Service:

Northern Region
Federal Building, Missoula, MT 59801

Southwestern Region
517 Gold Avenue, SW
Albuquerque, NM 87101

California Region
630 Sansome Street
San Francisco, CA 94111

Rocky Mountain Region
Federal Center
Building 85
Denver, CO 80225

Intermountain Region
324 25th Street
Ogden, UT 84401

Pacific Northwest Region
319 SW Pine Street
P. O. Box 3623
Portland, OR 97208

Eastern Region
710 North Sixth Street
Milwaukee, WI 53203

Southern Region
50 Seventh Street, NE
Atlanta, GA 30323

Alaska Region
Federal Office Building
Juneau, AK 99801

NATURAL AREAS ADMINISTERED BY THE NATIONAL PARK SERVICE

Acadia National Park, Maine. Rugged coastal area on Mount Desert Island, highest elevation on Eastern Seaboard; picturesque Schoodic Peninsula on mainland; half of Isle au Haut, exhibiting spectacular cliffs. Address: Route 1, Box 1, Bar Harbor, ME 04609.

Badlands National Monument, South Dakota. Ruggedly eroded layered sedimentary deposits containing great numbers of prehistoric animal fossils. Address: P. O. Box 72, Interior, SD 57750.

Bryce Canyon National Park, Utah. Contains perhaps the most colorful and unusual erosional forms in the world. In horseshoe-shaped amphitheaters along the edge of the Paunsaugunt Plateau of southern Utah stand innumerable highly colored and grotesque pinnacles, walls, and spires. Address: Bryce Canyon, UT 84717.

Cedar Breaks, National Monument, Utah. Huge natural amphitheater eroded into the variegated Pink Cliffs (Wasatch Formation), which are 2,000 feet thick at this point. Address: c/o Southern Utah Group, NPS, P. O. Box 749, Cedar City, UT 84720.

Colorado National Monument, Colorado. Sheer-walled canyons, towering monoliths, and weird formations hewed by erosion in sandstone. Address: c/o Curecant, National Recreation Area, 334 South 10th Street, Montrose, CO 81401.

Crater Lake National Park, Oregon. Lake of unique blue in heart of once-active volcano; encircled by multicolored lava walls 500 to 2,000 feet high. Address: c/o Klamath Falls Group, NPS, P. O. Box 128, Klamath Falls, OR 97601.

Craters of the Moon National Monument, Idaho. Fissure eruptions, volcanic cones, craters, lava flows, caves, and other volcanic phenomena; 43,243.00 acres designated as wilderness, October 23, 1970. Address: P. O. Box 29, Arco, ID 83213.

Dinosaur National Monument, Colorado, Utah. Spectacular canyons cut by Green and Yampa rivers through upfolded mountains. Quarry containing fossil remains of dinosaurs and other ancient animals. Federal acreage: 149,443.79 in Colorado, 49,637.03 in Utah. Address: P. O. Box 101, Dinosaur, CO 81610.

Glacier Bay National Monument, Alaska. Great tidewater glaciers and examples of early stages of postglacial forests; rare species of wildlife. Largest area in national park system. Address: c/o Alaska Group, NPS, P. O. Box 2252, Anchorage, AK 99501.

Glacier National Park, Montana. Superb Rocky Mountain scenery, with numerous glaciers and lakes among the highest peaks, forms part of the Waterton-Glacier International Peace Park established May 2, 1932. Address: West Glacier, MT 59936.

Grand Canyon National Monument, Arizona. Part of the Grand Canyon of the Colorado River containing Toroweap Point with its unusual view of the Inner Gorge and lava dam of recent era. Address: c/o Grand Canyon National Park, P. O. Box 129, Grand Canyon, AZ 86023.

Grand Teton National Park, Wyoming. Series of peaks comprising the most impressive part of the Teton Range; once a noted landmark of Indians and "mountain men." Includes part of Jackson Hole, winter feeding ground of largest American elk herd. A Living History area. Address: P. O. Box 67, Moose, WY 83012.

Kings Canyon National Park, California. Mountain wilderness dominated by two enormous canyons of the Kings River and by the summit peaks of the High Sierra. General Grant Grove (formerly General Grant National Park), with its giant sequoias, is a detached section of the park. Address: Three Rivers, CA 93271.

Lassen Volcanic National Park, California. Lassen Peak, only recently active volcano in conterminous United States, erupted between 1914 and 1921; impressive volcanic phenomena. A Living History area. Address: Mineral, CA 96063.

Mount McKinley National Park, Alaska. Mount McKinley, 20,320 feet, highest mountain in North America, large glaciers of the Alaska Range; caribou, Dall sheep, moose, grizzly bears, timber wolves, and other wildlife. Second-largest national park. A Living History area. Address: c/o Alaska Group, NPS, P. O. Box 2252, Anchorage, AK 99501.

Mount Rainier National Park, Washington. Greatest single-peak glacial system in the United States radiating from the summit and slopes of an ancient volcano; dense forests; subalpine flowered meadows. Address: Longmire, WA 98397.

North Cascades National Park, Washington. Wild alpine region of jagged peaks, mountain lakes, glaciers, plants and animal communities. Address: Sedro Woolley, WA 98284.

Olympic National Park, Washington. Mountain wilderness containing finest remains of Pacific Northwest rain forest; active glaciers, rare Roosevelt elk; Pacific shore. Address: 600 East Park Avenue, Port Angeles, WA 98362.

Rocky Mountain National Park, Colorado. Rich in scenery; Trail Ridge Road sightseeing on the Continental Divide; 107 named peaks over 11,000 feet; wildlife; wildflowers; 410 square miles of the Rockies Front Range. Address: Estes Park, CO 80517.

Sequoia National Park, California. Great groves of giant sequoias, world's largest and among the oldest living things; magnificent High Sierra scenery, including Mount Whitney (14,494 feet), highest mountain in contiguous United States. Address: Three Rivers, CA 93271.

Yellowstone National Park, Wyoming, Montana, Idaho. World's greatest geyser area, with about 3,000 geysers and hot springs; spectacular falls; Grand Canyon of the Yellowstone. Rich in wildlife. First and largest national park. Federal acreage: 2,039,216.98 in Wyoming; 149,031.90 in Montana; 31,488.00 in Idaho. Address: Yellowstone National Park, WY 82190.

Yosemite National Park, California. Mountainous region of unusual beauty seen from Tioga Road; Yosemite Valley and other inspiring gorges; nation's highest waterfall; three groves of giant sequoias; a Living History area. Address: P. O. Box 577, Yosemite National Park, CA 95389.

RECREATIONAL AREAS ADMINISTERED BY THE NATIONAL PARK SERVICE

Appalachian National Scenic Trail, Maine, New Hampshire, Vermont, Massachusetts, Connecticut, New York, Pennsylvania, Maryland, West Virginia, Tennessee, North Carolina, Georgia. A scenic trail of approximately 2,000 miles follows the Appalachian Mountains from Mount Katahdin, Maine, to Springer Mountain, Georgia. One of the two initial units of the national trail system. Federal acreage by state unavailable. Address: Northern Unit: c/o Regional Office, NPS, 143 South 3rd Street, Philadelphia, PA 19106; Southern Unit: c/o Regional Office, NPS, 3401 Whipple Avenue, Atlanta, GA 30344.

Bighorn Canyon National Recreation Area, Montana, Wyoming. A 71-mile-long reservoir created by Yellowtail Dam on the Bighorn River; extends 47 miles through spectacular Bighorn Canyon. The Crow Indian Reservation borders a large part of the area. Federal acreage: 33,548.00 in Montana; 28,438.00 in Wyoming. Address: c/o North Cascades National Park, Sedro Woolley, WA 98284.

Pictured Rocks National Lakeshore, Michigan. Superlative scenic area on Lake Superior with multicolored sandstone cliffs, broad beaches, bars, dunes, waterfalls, inland lakes, ponds, marshes, hardwood and coniferous forests, and numerous birds and animals. First national lakeshore. Land area, 65,568 acres. Address: c/o Isle Royale National Park, 87 North Ripley Street, Houghton, MI 49931.

Ross Lake National Recreation Area, Washington. Mountain-ringed reservoir in Skagit River Canyon, separating north and south units of North Cascades National Park. Address: c/o North Cascades National Park, Sedro Woolley, WA 98284.

St. Croix National Scenic Riverway, Wisconsin, Minnesota. About 200 miles of the beautiful St. Croix River and its Namekagon tributary. An initial component of the national wild and scenic rivers system. Federal acreage: 1,600.70 in Wisconsin; 95.22 in Minnesota. Address: P. O. Box 579, St. Croix Falls, WI 54024.

Shadow Mountain National Recreation Area, Colorado. Shadow Mountain Lake and Lake Granby, two units of the Colorado-Big Thompson Project, adjacent to the west entrance of Rocky Mountain National Park. Address: c/o Rocky Mountain Group, NPS, Estes Park, CO 80517.

Sleeping Bear Dunes National Lakeshore, Michigan. Notable for its beaches, massive sand dunes, forests, and lakes, two offshore islands, and Lake Michigan shore. Address: 400 Main Street, Frankfort, MI 49635.

Whiskeytown-Shasta-Trinity National Recreation Area, California. A scenic mountain region excellent for fishing, boating, and sightseeing at Whiskeytown Lake, formed by a dam across Clear Creek. The U. S. Forest Service, U. S. Department of Agriculture, administers 172,588-acre Shasta and Trinity-Lewistown units. Address: Whiskeytown Unit, P. O. Box 188, Whiskeytown, CA 96095.

Wolf National Scenic Riverway, Wisconsin. Twenty-four miles of fast water, ideal for canoeing, fishing, and scenic enjoyment. An initial component of the national wild and scenic rivers system. Address: c/o Chicago Field Office, NPS, 2510 Dempster Street, Room 214, Des Plaines, IL 60016.

INDEX